USING the
WORKSHOP
APPROACH
in the
HIGH SCHOOL
ENGLISH CLASSROOM

To my late grandfather Robert R. Rollins Sr.,
who pushed me to reach every student.

To my late grandmother Nellie Rollins,
for her belief that I ruled the world.

To my husband Bret,
for his patience, encouragement, and his ability to see this project
clearly when I could not.

To my daughter Anna Mackenzie Urbanski,
who wrote this book with me in the first year of her life.

To Karen Haag and Lil Brannon,
who never stopped believing.

To my students,
who teach and inspire me every day.

USING the WORKSHOP APPROACH in the HIGH SCHOOL ENGLISH CLASSROOM

Modeling Effective
Writing, Reading, and
Thinking Strategies
for Student Success

CYNTHIA D. URBANSKI

CORWIN PRESS
A SAGE Publications Company
Thousand Oaks, California

For information:

Corwin Press
A Sage Publications Company
2455 Teller Road
Thousand Oaks, California 91320
E-mail: order@corwinpress.com

Sage Publications Ltd.
1 Oliver's Yard
55 City Road
London EC1Y 1SP
United Kingdom

Sage Publications India Pvt. Ltd.
B-42, Panchsheel Enclave
Post Box 4109
New Delhi 110 017 India

Printed in the United States of America.

Library of Congress Cataloging-in-Publication Data

Urbanski, Cynthia D.
Using the workshop approach in the high school English classroom : modeling effective writing, reading, and thinking strategies for student success / Cynthia D. Urbanski.
        p. cm.
Includes bibliographical references and index.
ISBN 1-4129-2548-7 (cloth) — ISBN 1-4129-2549-5 (pbk.)
    1. English language—Composition and exercises—Study and teaching (Secondary) 2. Language arts (Secondary) I. Title.
LB1631.U73 2006
808'.042'0712—dc22
                                                    2005018385

This book is printed on acid-free paper.

05   06   07   08   09   10   9   8   7   6   5   4   3   2   1

Acquisitions Editor:	Kylee Liegl
Editorial Assistant:	Jaime Cuvier
Project Editor:	Tracy Alpern
Copy Editor:	Pam Suwinsky
Proofreader:	Penelope Sippel
Typesetter:	C&M Digitals (P) Ltd.
Indexer:	Ellen Slavitz
Cover Designer:	Michael Dubowe

Contents

Foreword

S logging through stacks of papers, camping out in trailers that are planted on what used to be the soccer field, trudging through file cabinets looking for that important handout that has now magically disappeared, stamping out every single misplaced comma or misspelled word—these well-worn pathways to teaching are often the ones that cause us to burn out. If you are like me, you are always looking for new, exciting adventures, new terrain to investigate, new roads to travel, new avenues that will make our classrooms, once again, come alive with learning. Cindy Urbanski's volume is our guide to this exciting adventure. This book offers new ways of engaging with writing and literature. She asks that we become coaches, modeling our reading and writing strategies for our students so that they can see, firsthand, how we think about literature or compose an essay.

Coaches. When Cindy asked me to read an early version of this book, I tried to persuade her to ditch the "coaching" metaphor. My associations with coaches (that is, before Cindy) had not been all positive. Now I don't speak about coaches in a vacuum. I don't tell many people this, but I had a state championship team in Class B girls' basketball when I taught high school in Texas. I don't tell many people, because I may be the only winning coach in the entire state of Texas who didn't become a principal. And so my association with coaches—the ones who were given the history classes, who were the disciplinarians, and later became the principals—did not, on the surface, seem to speak to the teacher I wanted to be. But Cindy's gifts as a writer and teacher convinced me otherwise. She saw from her experience a different world, where modeling and showing—not telling and then saying it again louder—was the image for teaching writing and literature that we teachers could enact. She could see in her own experience as a runner and a cross-country coach and as a writer and as a teacher of writing how those worlds come together and make the classroom a vibrant and productive place.

Coaching. If you are wondering, "How am I supposed to model and show students my writing and reading?" "Am I supposed to expose all my false starts at writing—all my dead ends?" don't worry. This volume reminds us that even teachers struggle with their reading and writing. By showing our students the work behind the finished product, we demystify how reading and writing can mutually enrich our understanding of what we read and our engagement with what we write. It will give you courage to work along with your students, to build your classroom as a writing and reading workshop.

Coaching. As a "coach," I can speak to my students about how a book touched me in personal and profound ways. As a reader, I can show students how I make personal connections to literature or connect my responses to literature to the world at large. Take, for example, this short piece I wrote for my class after reading Cindy's book:

> On the 24-hour flight to Taipei, after watching all four cross-Pacific movies, I pulled a novel from my bag. Anita had given me this book and inscribed in its cover, "To Lil, for growing up in the South." I had this book for over a year. *The Secret Lives of Bees* began to melt the remaining hours in my hands, taking me home to a life I had known, but never lived, a life far removed from mine, to a girl who needed to know her mother, her mother's love left to her in secrets that she could never fully unravel. At 2 a.m. somewhere over the Taiwan Straits, where missiles perch on tanks awaiting Chinese children's cries for independence, for freedom, for easing of the iron hand, for the space that an island carves from a cold enveloping sea, I saw that I, too, longed to know: Had I in my struggles to teach, cloaked my subject in secrets, found my space, and left the child to cry alone on the dusty road?

My personal connection between the plight of Lily in the novel as she worked through the tragic loss of her mother and the plight of Taiwanese and mainland Chinese children who, in their own ways, struggle for freedom and for their motherland, demonstrates to my students how my reading of a novel portraying life in South Carolina in 1964 could resonate in my imagination to world struggles in 2005. As a writer, I could show my students how repetition propels my meaning forward. I could even show them several endings to the paragraph that I drafted before I arrived at this one, the final one, for now.

Cindy's imaginative energy and creativity for teaching reading, writing, thinking, and literature (with both a little *l* and a big *L*) show us ways of connecting with our students while still helping them tackle the end-of-the-year test without leaving any child on the dusty road.

I must admit that my not unusual failure to connect to all of my students is featured within these pages. I remember well the class Cindy talks about—a class full of teachers who were struggling to do well by their students and who were searching for ways to engage their students and still manage to have them well prepared for the writing test at the end of the school year. I gave them theory, when they needed to have a way to bring theory and practice together. When I talked about practice, they thought I had no idea about the classroom world they inhabited. They were being left in the dust, and I felt like a card-carrying member of the "research establishment"—*those people* who were asking questions about stuff that no teacher even cared about, things like, "What was the spelling variability in the flash condition?"

Cindy saw beyond my shortcomings and found what she needed in her journey to create in all of her students a love for reading and writing. This volume documents her journey to integrate the teaching of literature with best practices in the teaching of writing. It tells her teaching story of working with rural kids in North Carolina and with inner-city students in the Charlotte/Mecklenburg schools. It is a powerful teacher narrative based on classroom research and reflection that documents not only what she does in the classroom but how and why she engages her students in the ways she describes here.

This book, clearly the work of a master teacher, shows those of us who struggle to get our acts together in the classroom, to integrate the teaching of reading, writing, literature, even grammar, by showing students that they are thinkers and knowers and storytellers. Cindy models for us in the same way she models for her students, letting us see her and her students at work, showing us how she arrives at her beliefs and values, and demonstrating her thinking and learning processes as a writer, reader, runner, and teacher.

I am excited that we teachers now have this book as a guide, because in reading it we embark on a very interesting and exciting journey. We are taken into classrooms and shown how to transform our own practices in ways that we might not have before imagined. Cindy's book surely gives me the courage to teach in new ways and to begin again in ways that will enable each student to embark on the journey with me. In other words, this book puts Cindy Urbanski's teaching on the map.

Lillian Brannon
University of North Carolina at Charlotte

Acknowledgments

Corwin Press gratefully acknowledges the contributions of the following reviewers:

Elizabeth Liberti
Secondary Reading
  Specialist
Regional Coordinator
Williamson County Schools
Franklin, TN

Sue Reed
English Teacher
Trenton High School
Trenton, FL

Kim C. Romero, NBCT
English Teacher
Jack Britt High School
Cumberland County, NC

Elise Wajid
Reading First
NJ Department of Education
Sewell, NJ

Gordon Dasher
Classroom Teacher
Trenton High School
Trenton, FL

Denise Beasley
English, Journalism, Writing
  Teacher
Osseo Fairchild High School
Osseo, WI

About the Author

Cynthia D. Urbanski is a Co-Leader of the University of North Carolina-Charlotte Writing Project, where her focus is teacher research, summer institutes, and structuring professional development for surrounding areas. Since graduating from the North Carolina Teaching Fellows Program at UNC–Chapel Hill in 1995 and while completing a master's of English education at UNC-Charlotte in 2000, she has worked with writers from middle grades through the undergraduate level. As an instructor at North Mecklenburg High School since 2000, she has worked with student writers in the International Baccalaureate Program as well as standard-level English courses. Her mission has been to help all students improve their literacy skills by making their writing, reading, and thinking meaningful to them. She continues to run regularly and considers it an integral part of her writing process and her life. Currently she is working to develop the concept of her second book project and spending time with her family in Charlotte, North Carolina.

C H A P T E R   O N E

Running and Writing

I may never have the words to describe a good run. Especially the feeling when I finish and the sweat cools on my back, forehead, and arms, the fresh, cool air is still pumping through my lungs, the blood is pumping through my body, and my tired muscles quiver uncontrollably. It is a special kind of afterglow.

Then there is the mental triumph, the feeling of accomplishment that comes with pushing my body for 5 more minutes and then 10. The mind clears, stress dissolves, problems are solved, and the soul is at peace. Along with that comes the realization that the person who once said, "I only run when someone is chasing me," is the same person who just sailed through the neighborhood with her 80-pound dog in tow.

It has occurred to me lately that writing and running have quite a bit in common. Both take dedication and practice, and both abilities disappear if they are not used. Running is always hard for me in the beginning. I stand at the end of my driveway, Doc, my yellow lab, wagging his tail and ready to take off like a bullet. I look up the hill and think about the miles ahead of me. Taking a long breath, I put one foot in front of the other, and I am off. About halfway up the hill, my heart starts to pound, my lungs start to burst, and my legs begin to cramp. I think, "I will never make it up this hill, much less the 2 1/2 miles left ahead of me."

The stretch of pavement ahead is the blank page that must be filled with writing. I sit before my computer screen, staring at the picture of a moose with shaggy hair on my desktop, knowing that when I click on the Word icon, a blank white screen will be staring at *me*. I finally drag my mouse over, double click, and there it is. I start to type one or two words, and they are truly horrible. My pulse quickens, my brain cramps, and I think, "I will never be able to write the first three lines, much less fill 10 pages."

I begin to think, "Okay. I'll just run (or write) until I can't possibly run one more step (or write one more word)." The pain in my legs and brain is searing, and I am sure that the next step or word will be my last. I know that my husband will come home to find me lying in the street or crumpled on my desk. However, that step is not my last, nor is that word, and suddenly I'm not thinking about the pain any more. My legs and brain stop cramping. I'm running without thinking, I'm writing what I'm thinking. Words fill the screen and the miles fall away. I'm flying.

Sometimes when I run, I never achieve flight. Each step is painful. By the second mile, I've had it, and I walk home disappointed and sour. I talk to myself, saying, "Today, I did not have a good run. But I did run; that is something. I built a little muscle today, and that will help me tomorrow when I run again. After all, even two slow, painful miles is better than sitting on the couch watching TV."

Sometimes when I write, my words never take flight. I sit and painfully churn out several pages of what I know is pure garbage. My thoughts refuse to come together, and the pain in my brain never goes away. I get very little accomplished in the time that I allotted that day for writing. I tell myself, "At least I wrote, and I have built a few good ideas in the pile of pages I have created. Those can be used tomorrow when I sit down to write again."

When I finish a good run, I am exhilarated, but dog-tired. I'm sweaty and worn out, but I'm also pumped up. I can't possibly rest. When I finish a good piece of writing, my eyes are blurry from staring at it and my hair is standing up all over my head. My brain feels like a big pile of mush, but I can't rest. I am totally exhilarated. In both instances, as I bask in the afterglow, I think to myself, "Now why did I dread this so much, why did I get so discouraged? I know the reward for sticking this out!" I can never answer the question. I can only vow to continue to push myself again and again.

Many people have misconceptions about writing. Dr. Sam Watson of the University of North Carolina at Charlotte loves to tell his students that "writing is not sitting in the garret with a skull on the desk beside you, furiously filling up pages with brilliant ideas. It is the act of putting pen to paper; it is an action, and something we *do*. It is work!" I must add to that statement that writing is not sitting in a sunny room with the spring breeze blowing from an open window while you tap out brilliant and perfectly formed ideas. Indeed, at this moment, I am in such a room and I am attempting to type, struggling to strain my thoughts through my fingers and willing my hand to write.

People do not expect to go out and run the Boston Marathon without training. They do not expect to run even a mile when they have never run more than the two steps it takes to get in front of someone in the fast food line. Why would they expect to sit down and write the great American novel if they have never before spent time trying to compose?

People can easily be convinced that there are some tricks to running. Holding your head, your arms, and your body in the right position helps tremendously. Focusing on your breathing to keep it as even and as deep as possible will get rid of cramps. So why would people not expect there to be a few writing tricks that could get a person over the tough spots? It is accepted that there are good days and bad days in running, so why would writing be any different?

People know that running is painful. They see the runners in marathons sweating, limping, and throwing up. They know these people are highly trained. Writing is a very similar process. Those who do it every day limp and sweat and get sick over their work, but like runners, they keep at it because they know that there will be a reward at the end.

People do not know these things about writing because they do not understand writing in the same way that they understand running. Their understanding of writing, like most other things, comes out of their own experience, and for most people that means the experience they had in school. Our students' parents expect their children's writing instruction to be similar to their own. They expect to see papers marked to the *nth* degree for spelling and grammar. They expect their children to write five-paragraph essays, each paragraph containing a topic sentence and three supporting sentences.

The teacher down the hall preaches such a form and wields a red pen should any unlucky student create a faux pas as he writes. Students are given an assignment with cursory comments about drafting and revising and are expected to turn in a finished product at the appointed time. Anyone seeking the guidance of another student will be punished for cheating, and the teacher will not read and comment on drafts because that would be giving students the answer. The paper will be graded, and the grade will be recorded for all time in the grade book. Some teachers may store the writing assignment in a folder of some sort that will be given to the student at the end of the year. In most cases the folder will be thrown away or placed in a remembrance box under a bed. The writing accomplished in such settings is almost never revisited or revised after it is graded, and rarely is it used for any real purpose other than as part of the justification for a final grade in a course.

As teachers who are under the gun of public scrutiny, it seems as if we should adopt the practices of "the teacher down the hall." We want to challenge our students. We want to get them ready for the real world and for college. If we make things too easy for them—and many are convinced that the process approach does just that—we are letting them down. However, such practices and methods do not allow students to have bad writing days with which to build writing muscle, and they seldom give students a chance to fly. More important, these methods are not realistic. Professional writers describe a process that is much more like that of the runner. (Donald Murray's *Shoptalk* [1990] logs many such thoughts.)

> *If it turns out to be a novel, then I will have wanted to write a novel. But if it turns out to be stories, it'll turn out that that's what I wanted to do.*
>
> —Grace Paley

> *I remember that I started writing* Sleepless Nights *because of a single line. The line was: "Now I will start my novel, but I don't know whether to call myself I or she."*
>
> —Elizabeth Hardwick

What civilians do not understand—and to a writer anyone not a writer is a civilian—is that writing is manual labor of the mind: a job, like laying pipe.

—John Gregory Dunne

Writing is hard work that follows no form. The stories and thoughts carry the writer along if she is astute enough to hear them and disciplined enough to follow them. The notion of writing carrying the writer through the text she is creating is similar to the way a runner's legs seem to take over and propel the body forward.

THE WORKSHOP CULTURE: A STUDY OF COACHING

To create a picture of the workshop-based classroom, let's return for a moment to our running and writing image and carry it a bit further. Imagine sitting a track team down in a classroom and lecturing them on the finer points of running for competition and then holding them to these practices, perhaps taking away points for every so-called "mistake" of form, even when the "mistake" allowed them to run faster. We would not expect to have a successful season under these circumstances.

What if we coached the team by offering them advice from what we know about running and have continued to learn through reading all of the latest running magazines? What if we offered this knowledge in bits and pieces as we watched the students run? The things we suggested would be contingent upon our observations of the runners and our assessment of what they needed. We would expect to model the ways we wanted the runner to hold her head. We would *show* her how to use her arms to make her way up a challenging hill. We would then watch closely as the runner tried to emulate our actions, offering encouragement, praise, and more suggestions all the while. I think we could expect quite a bit of success if we were to use this approach to running instruction.

Let's continue with our ideas for coaching running for a bit. We would run with our athletes. Maybe not as far or as fast as our best runners, but they would see us out there sweating and work-ing along with them. We would run in order to keep our own run-ning muscles active, to model what real runners do when they encounter real problems, and maybe, most important, to remind ourselves of what it feels like to be out of breath, to get cramps, and to hit "the wall."

We would expect our runners to do much more than perform on the day of the race. We would expect these young runners to practice under our supervision. We realize that, if we expect them to improve, we need to push them each day in practice, when they can focus on their form and stamina without worrying about the outcome. Surely on non-race days the students could run on their own without us watching them, but our very presence pushes them to try a little harder and grow a little more while ensuring that they will have much-needed encouragement when they think they cannot possibly run another step.

And that's when we would step in to help. "Coach, I always get a cramp in my right calf on the last mile; what can I do about that?" "Coach, I think I twisted my ankle." "Coach, I don't feel well and I'm just so hot." We are expected to know how to respond to all of these complaints so that the runner can continue to improve and excel. By being there, we can help them to push through their discouragement and pain.

Also, in practice, we encourage, cajole, and even require our athletes to step out of their comfort zones and try new things. We know that stretching prevents injury, so we require that. We encour-age and require our runners to experiment with different warm-ups so that they can find what is best for them. We help our runners to build muscle and stamina in practice that they will need in the race. Practice rarely emulates the race; it simply pre-pares the athletes for that performance.

When time for the performance comes, we trust the runners to know what they need to do. If we had a runner who always ran best when she wore green socks, we would allow that. We would also allow the other team members not to wear green socks if such attire did not help their running in any way. As running coaches, we would be accepting, within reason, of what our kids prove to us helps them improve their athletic ability. For instance, green socks are not a problem, but we would never allow a runner to begin a meet without warming up because of the damage we know it can cause. On race day we must step back and watch closely. A good coach notes what a runner does for a meet, so that success can be repeated and failure can be altered and improved upon. The coach is the careful observer at this point.

What would happen if we followed such a model for writing instruction? It seems a little bizarre at first; teachers simply do not act this way. So why does the word *teaching* not bring forth the image of the kind of instruction we have described? For some of us, the word *coach* may not have even called up this scenario. A "coach" may be a large man with a protruding belly and baseball cap, blowing his whistle at kids and spitting tobacco juice. In writing this book using a coaching metaphor, I was concerned at first about the way people—especially serious teachers—perceive coaches. As a high school teacher and cross-country coach, I found that there was a very clear distinction between teachers who coached and coaches who taught. I wanted to be the former. But I also wanted other teachers to coach, and in doing that redefine both words, giving each more strength, power, and prestige. I want to dispel the myth of that overweight coach, but more so the myth of the teacher as the pinch-faced crone with a red pen and a full three-ring binder, standing behind a podium, droning on endlessly to students and then requiring them to regurgitate the information. I want to create the image of adults working continually to gain knowledge themselves and then working with children to help them find their own reasons for learning.

Sadly, English teachers seem to fall into the crone category a little more readily than teachers of other subjects. Every time someone new finds out that I teach English, they say, "Well, I'd better stop talking before you have to correct my grammar." Or, "Ugh! I hated English." They always look a little frightened for the rest of the visit, as if I may whip out my red pen at any moment and begin writing big fat F's on their foreheads. Such adverse reactions make me sad, because we are the people who get to teach the fun curriculum. We are the ones who get to explore life with our students. We are in the position to help them discover how they think and what they feel. We can watch them explore the gold mine of their own ideas and experience the beauty of ideas around them. We get to demonstrate the power of words and, by learning to experiment with words, the power that they themselves possess. We can help them discover flight.

We cannot show our students how to fly from our exalted position behind the podium. Students can never experience flight trapped inside a formulaic box. We have to come around to their side, push up our sleeves, and work right along with them. We have to model writing and thinking and reading for comprehension and enjoyment. We have to watch them closely so that we can nudge them when they need it. We must stay abreast of the latest findings in writing instruction so that we may best know how to nudge them. We have to praise and encourage and cheer. We have to allow them to practice under our supervision, and we have to allow for meaningful performance. Most of all, we must give our students real and meaningful experiences that make them want to write. We have to get them stirred up over something more than a grade if we ever expect them to take risks and grow. We must coach them.

We have to allow for their differences by meeting and teaching each child at his level and then challenging him to move past it. We cannot force structure or style, and we must enable our students to become confident and fluent; then we enable them to choose the appropriate style for what they want to say. Nor can we dictate the process that each writer goes through in order to reach the final destination.

CONCLUSIONS AND MISSION

In many ways, this is another book about teaching writing, but there is one key way in which it is very different. Donald Graves (1991, 1996), Lucy Calkins (1986), Nancy Atwell (1987), and countless others have written wonderful books about writing workshops for elementary and middle grades. I have learned quite a bit from these teachers, and you will see them mentioned often in this book. But, these books do not really deal with high school curriculum. Tom Romano's book (1987) does deal with teaching writing in high school, but only two chapters deal with writing in and among literature. My hope is to take good writing instruction and explain how it works hand in hand with good reading instruction, thereby helping teachers institute real writing instruction into their literature-based classrooms.

So you see, my aim is not to trivialize the teaching of writing by comparing it to coaching. My aim is to empower both teachers and students to work together in the high school classroom to ensure that students master and understand the power in their own voices and feel confident in showing that voice to the world in their writing. But in order to do that, we must also give them control over their own thinking, reading, and thinking about what they read. And at the very foundation of this aim is the unwavering belief that all children can learn to write, just as all can learn to run. We've all seen people in wheelchairs racing around the track. Children will learn to write when we teach them to run. As they become stronger, they will run fast enough to fly.

Chapter Two

Who Writes the Rule Book Anyway?

*Accountability, Tests,
and the History of Rhetoric*

Before we plunge headlong into the development of the workshop-based classroom, we must deal with a bit of information about our society's view of writing and how we got there. Just yesterday my students received their PSAT scores back. It was a pretty exciting day, considering that this PSAT was based on the new, 2005 SAT that includes writing and grammar. The top 13 students, with scores ranging from 220 to 200, have one thing in common. They are all readers and writers. They spend a good deal of time outside of school in this endeavor. The *really* interesting thing is that the top scorer reads and studies old and new rock lyrics and writes his own songs in his spare time. He has a band that plays pretty regularly in local clubs. The number 2 scorer is really into young adult fantasy literature. Often, instead of doing assigned homework, she reads or writes her own fantasy. She also spends a good deal of time writing for Fanfiction.org, and she and her friends spend hours reading and critiquing each other's work. So how do we get from these awesome, creative kids to a typical English class today that deals mainly with test prep and formula writing?

A BIT OF HISTORY

I keep a collection of quotes from writers (from Donald Murray's *Shoptalk*, 1990) on the wall beside my desk at school. I keep them there to remind myself and my students of how messy real writing is and how different it is from the nice neat formulas that I was taught and used to teach. I keep them there to remind myself that I am training thinkers, not test takers.

So where do we get these ideas about writing instruction if not from the people who actually write? The myth is that we get them from Aristotle. Aristotle wrote his *Rhetoric,* and Cicero developed it for the Romans, but the ancients' ideas of composing were largely for oratorical purposes. Aristotle, and the Romans who would later adopt and adapt his principles, were addressing the learned few who needed to impart their knowledge to others by means of oratorical or written communication. The patterns that a speaker chose were based on his knowledge of the audience he was speaking to and his reasons for sharing his knowledge. Though people did have a need to compose speeches, the art of oratory was considered much more important than the act of writing.

Through the rise and fall of the Roman Empire, the height of the Middle Ages, and the rebirth of the arts and sciences of the Renaissance, Aristotle's *Rhetoric* remained the foundation for the field of study that took the name of his book. Though it was ignored for hundreds of years at a time, while more pressing matters such as defending one's life and property from barbarians took precedence, its concepts survived.

By the 19th century (and, yes, we are making quite a jump here), a morphing of Aristotle's ideas began to occur. This morphing is what has caused much of our current confusion in writing instruction, in my opinion. In the name of ancient Western tradition, textbook writers as early as 1875 were coming up with orderly forms for writing called "modes of discourse." We recognize ideas such as narrative, descriptive, and expository modes in our own classrooms today. Aristotle never mentioned such modes, but as academics struggled for a way to teach new students to write so that they could move on to what were felt to be more important areas of study—such as the sciences or business—these categories became increasingly popular (Conners, 1981, p. 447). Conners sums up the onset of the modes by saying, "The modes became popular and stayed popular because they fit into the abstract, mechanical nature of writing instruction at the time . . ." (p. 453). The focus of writing instruction shifted from Aristotle's ideas of audience and purpose to the idea of making one's ideas fit into a preconstructed mold. People were looking for a writing course that would prepare young men for any type of writing they might have to do in life, no matter their major or occupation. Writing came to be viewed as a utilitarian skill rather than an art form.

The teaching of writing came to be placed into the dusty dregs of the English Department. Only the lesser and inexperienced scholars were sentenced to the thankless job of teaching people to write, and with hard work and study they hoped to some day have that sentence repealed. At the university, composition classes were seen as remediation. The prevailing attitude was, if a person is coming to university, he should be able to write. Writing was something that must be taught at the college level only because high school teachers failed to do it. The people teaching composition were generally not trained in the study of writing, but rather the study of literature, and therefore were more susceptible to ideas such as the modes and later the five-paragraph theme as they searched for ways to improve student writing. Such ideas represent writing as something that can be nicely broken down into neat categories and structured steps and therefore passed on to students as absolute knowledge, a solid framework in which to plug in thoughts, and never to be deviated from. This lack of deviation is precisely the problem with modes, according to Knoblauch and Brannon (1997):

> Too many teachers, like their ancient predecessors, view genres as rigid structures that must be learned precisely and then never violated if writing is to be coherent, organized, and effective. Too many believe that learning to write is equivalent to learning these structures, that teaching writing means insisting on formal correctness, that tidying up the surface of discourse causes the maturation of writers. The consequence has been to promote a ceremonial view of discourse among students, a belief that writing is mainly a process of honoring the conventions that matter to English teachers rather than a process of discovering personal meaning, thinking well in language, or achieving serious intellectual purposes. (p. 31)

If a student's idea does not fit into the framework, it is not useful or important. It is simply lost. The message is that any idea that doesn't fit in the box is worthless and a waste of time.

In the end, the idea of modes was exploded because it was found that they did not actually teach people how to write. Albert Kitzhaber writes:

> The forms of discourse were ideally suited to the purpose of instruction in a subject that had been cut off from all relation with other subjects in the curriculum and, in a sense, from life itself. . . . They represent an unrealistic view of the writing process; a view that assumes writing is done by formula and in a social vacuum. They turn the attention of both teacher and student toward an academic exercise instead of toward a meaningful act of communication in social context. (Quoted in Conners, 1981, p. 454)

The modes didn't work because they have nothing to do with what real writers do. I particularly like the way that Kitzhaber refers to modes instruction as an "academic exercise." Those words bring up images of purple mimeographed worksheets and students dutifully filling in the blanks while teachers tell them that they are writing. James Kinneavy goes on to describe how distinction between modes has nothing to do with the writing process:

> A stress on modes of discourse rather than aims of discourse is a stress on "what" is being talked about rather than on "why" a thing is talked about. This is actually a substitute of means for ends. Actually, something is narrated for a reason. Narration, as such, is not a purpose. (Quoted in Conners, 1981, p. 454)

The modes ignored the fact that writing first comes from ideas and purpose. The form the writing takes depends on the best way to get that idea or purpose across to the audience. Deciding on a mode of discourse before deciding on an idea takes away the basic reason for writing to begin with—getting a purpose across to an audience.

People do not often think in structured steps. Students are hurt when they are not allowed to think outside of the box.

Their thoughts can never take flight if we do not open the lid. Writing is thinking on paper, and formulas and modes squelch that thinking. Why would we teach children to write in a way that is not consistent with the way real writers write? In my case, it was because I had not been taught to think about how real writers write. I had been taught the modes and the five-paragraph theme, and so, that is what I taught my students. I didn't sit down to think about my own composing process until I began graduate school. It was there that I was freed from the modes, and my own writing improved dramatically. As teachers, we must be aware of the history of writing instruction if we are to make informed decisions about the way we teach. I have touched on it briefly here, but I strongly recommend that writing teachers read the books and articles listed in the Suggested Reading at the end of this chapter. You may be surprised at what you find. I know I was.

AND WHAT ABOUT THE OTHER PARTS OF MY CURRICULUM?

"Alright already," you may be saying at this point. "All of this talk about writing is very nice and seems to make sense, but you forget about all of the literature I have to teach. Maybe I would have time for the 'coaching' in a creative writing class, but I have a curriculum to cover. When are you going to talk about literature? What about all of the tests that the state requires?" Let me begin to address that question in the form of a story—the story of how I came to write this book in the first place.

In the fall of 1999 I was just getting into my master's program and was for the first time really beginning to see how much I needed to learn. Sixteen hours into my course work, it was becoming obvious that taking a year off to study was the best thing I ever did for my prospective students. I was in a course called "Context and Issues in the Teaching of English" with a group of other experienced high school teachers, taught by Dr. Lil Brannon and Dr. Sam Watson. By October, the 6:30–9:30 class was really starting to wear on our nerves, and many of my classmates were staring down the barrel of the tenth grade writing test given by the state of North Carolina. I felt my own anxiety rising right along with theirs. That tenth grade test had consumed my teaching and had eventually driven me into sabbatical.

Tensions were certainly running high. Dr. Brannon had been trying to explain why practices like teaching the five-paragraph theme and modes of discourse were erroneous and hurtful to students. During our discussions, the continual reference by much of the class to how they had been taught to write, along with the formula writing that they felt was absolutely necessary to teach if their students were going to pass the writing test, reinforced what Conners (1981), Fort (1971), and Hairston (1982) were saying in the articles I mentioned earlier in this chapter. Still, many of the teachers were finding the new information hard to swallow, and the fact that their curriculum was literature based, as was the writing test, made many feel that teaching writing without formulas or modes was not at all feasible. I was having trouble swallowing that same pill myself, but I had recently come to see that I had been hurting my own students in the same way I had been hurt as a writer. We were all conscientious teachers who were trying to do what was best for our students. To think that we had been operating under a prevailing false system was unconscionable. It didn't help matters that the professor who used our classroom before we did was teaching the five-paragraph theme and left evidence of this on the board each time we met!

Finally, on the night before the state writing test, about two months into the course, things came to a head. Dr. Watson, the co-professor of our class, had also been teaching an expository writing class that semester. We had been given a week to read over and think about some of the reflections students in his expository writing class had written, so that we could discuss them, and along with that, what we saw happening in his expository writing class.

Dr. Brannon attempted to get the discussion started by asking someone who had taken Dr. Watson's expository class to talk about it. Before Dr. Brannon could begin, another student asked Dr. Brannon, "If teaching the five-paragraph theme is so wrong, why is it on the board right there?" Dr. Brannon's reply echoed Conners's article: "Just because people are teaching on the college level does not necessarily mean that they know how to teach *writing*. Most likely their training and research has been in the study and criticism of literature."

An attack on Dr. Brannon's philosophies of writing instruction ensued. The argument from the class was that her ideas of letting students find the form appropriate to the topic they were writing about was fine and dandy in elementary and middle school, and even in Dr. Watson's expository writing class, but high school was a whole different ball game. Many teachers felt that the amount of literature that had to be covered on the high school level made it impossible to teach writing in the way Dr. Brannon was describing. In addition, these students would be required to take the tenth grade writing test, in which they would need to answer a question that required literary analysis of a piece of world literature. Furthermore, we had found that if we taught students to follow a specific pattern, they would pass the test; in many cases, passing the test was a requirement for moving on to the next grade level, not to mention important to the school's status in North Carolina's accountability program. In short, it would be nice to be able to teach writing in the way Dr. Brannon was describing, but we just didn't have time for that in high school. It was a time for serious writing about literature.

We never got around to discussing Dr. Watson's expository writing class, and many of the teachers in our own class made a conscious decision just to survive until the end. Hallway conversations revealed that a few felt that the professors were completely out of touch with what the teachers had to deal with in the high school setting.

Because the state writing test seemed to be what was creating the barrier for the class, Dr. Brannon and Dr. Watson asked two experienced teachers to come speak to us about how they were dealing with the test without teaching formula writing. Though they offered some brilliant ideas about focusing on thinking skills, as well as real reading and writing strategies, some of the teachers in the class were still not convinced of what was becoming more and more clear to me. We had been operating under an outdated system with no real reasoning behind our practice other than "that's the way we were taught." In fact, those few teachers could not really see the difference between what the presenters were doing and their own methods of instruction.

The initial negative reactions of our class and those few who never changed their view of what our professors were trying to teach us piqued my interest. I knew for a fact that they were not bad teachers. I knew that every teacher in that room genuinely cared about his students and the students' growth. The teachers and their students were simply victims of an outdated system. I also knew how hard it was to break away from that system. Had I not experienced the benefits of the type of writing instruction Dr. Brannon spoke of with my own writing just a few months earlier in the National Writing Project Summer Institute, I would have been right there with the naysayers.

As I worked through my master's program, that experience stayed in the back of my mind. I returned to my high school classroom feeling empowered as a teacher. My students and I embarked on a grand adventure at the beginning of the year and emerged better thinkers, readers, and writers. I thought again of my colleagues from that fated class, as well as others I had met who mirrored their philosophies. I wanted to give those teachers the power, freedom, and joy I found in my own writing and reading and through that, my teaching, when I let go of formula writing and comprehension questions about what we read.

TESTING AND ACCOUNTABILITY

Even with all of this information, the facts remain the same. No matter what grade level we teach, no matter what wonderful educational program our schools have adopted in what beautiful part of the country, we all have one thing in common: testing and accountability. Whenever I am asked to do in-service for a school, whenever I do workshops for conferences, whenever I talk to other teachers anywhere, they want to know what I do about the test.

For the majority of my career I have taught tenth grade English, a.k.a. the most tested subject in North Carolina. My students take the PSAT in the fall, the writing test in March, and the comprehensive reading and math exam in May. In all honesty, as the years go on, I ignore the tests for the most part. I do not think that education is about a number on an exam taken on one day; I do not judge myself as a teacher solely based on test scores of my students, and I do not allow my students to judge themselves in that way either. I became a better teacher and a much happier person when I let go of the "report card." In no way do I want this to be a book about testing, but it is the elephant in the room, so let's deal with it here.

Testing is a reality. Our job as educators is certainly to prepare our students for these tests, but to protect them as well. The easiest way to prepare students is through drilling the test. If a teacher studies every nuance of her assessment and its scoring, and then diligently pours all of that information into her students' heads while at the same time motivating the students, her students will succeed. I know; I've done it.

But what if the test changes, or something about it was unanticipated by the teacher? What if a question seems totally different from any of the zillion practice questions the students have had experience with? What if, heaven forbid, students are placed in a nontesting situation where they have to read and write in real life, with *no* prompting questions or for a different audience? Disaster! I know; I've seen it.

Drilling the test is like training my cross-country team to one course in one type of weather. I would get awesome results for that race and misery for others. The whole idea is ludicrous.

At the same time, with all of the pressure put on educators by the No Child Left Behind Act for passing test scores, asking teachers to abandon a sure thing is a tall order. It's easy to sit back and say that drilling is educationally unsound when it isn't *your* future and the future of *your* students on the line. The year I returned to the classroom and implemented the workshop-based curriculum that I describe in this book. I did not address the state writing test my students were scheduled to take in the first week in March until the last week of January. Periodically, I would wake up in the middle of the night in a cold sweat. My previous writing test scores were a major reason I was hired to that position, and I had 122 students taking that test. I stuck to my guns only because I had come to a point in my life where if teaching that test was to be my job, I was going to have to change careers. If I was fired for test scores, I would have the satisfaction of knowing that I had taught my students to think and to write.

I took the same cavalier attitude toward the reading comprehensive test. For both tests, I started working exposure to the test and how to apply to the test what we had learned so far that year into my 10-minute mini-lessons each day for 3 to 4 weeks before the test. The other 80 minutes of each class period were spent with our regular workshop curriculum. I used the mini-lessons to expose the students to the nuances of both of the state assessments, and the students picked up on them much more quickly because of all they had learned about real reading and real writing. When the scores came back, my students soared above the state, district, and school averages.

After that year, I relaxed a bit. I felt much better about the time I had spent with my students, and I could tell at the end of the year that they really had made great strides in their reading, writing, and thinking. They were not churning out meaningless formulaic writing, as my students had in the past. They were writing thought-ful, varied pieces, the form of which depended on the audience the student wanted to reach as well as the overall purpose. They were reading and then thinking about and discussing what they read rather than searching for answers to questions. They were even coming up with questions themselves. Better yet, for the first time ever, many of them were enjoying English class and felt as if they were really getting a lot out of it because they had written pieces that they were proud of and had become connected to much that they had read.

Since then, our writing test has completely changed, and so has the SAT. These changes have been a blessing in disguise. First of all, with little idea about what this new test would look like or how it would be scored, it was difficult to teach to the test even if I wanted to. It kept me honest. Also, we had the blessing of a pilot year. The test counted for absolutely nothing, so I was free to experiment, with no pressure. I didn't talk about the test at all until 2 weeks before, when we looked at a few sample essays pro-vided by our school system. My students worked together in small groups to take apart the models and see how the authors had put them together. It was a great review for studying literature, and the students then knew what this state audience expected of them. I did require that each student do some prewriting and write a draft before putting their final copy on the test paper. The scores were again comparable with those of my friends' students who had been drilled.

The pilot year has truly solidified what I've known in my heart all along. If we teach students to think about what they read and write, and approach writing as writers, all of the assessment stuff takes care of itself. As they explore the works of other writers in search of new techniques to add to their own, students become true critical readers. We don't have to rail against the system or spend hours drafting letters to the state department about substandard grading. That is a waste of time and energy. I know. I've done it.

We simply teach good writing and reading and let it go. And then we help our students to realize that tests are important and that they should do their best. Tests are no problem if I have created a culture of learning in my classroom, but we must remember—and help our students to remember—that tests are not really a measure of who they are as people or learners. They are simply tests.

CONCLUSIONS

From the beginning, writing has been an art form, and like most forms of art, writing requires discipline and inspiration if one intends to create something worthwhile. The trouble comes when writing is viewed as a skill that all should come to possess, and with that view the search for a foolproof method to teach it. It's much like a paint-by-numbers approach to oil painting. What would happen if art classes came to have a state assessment? Yikes!

In each chapter that follows there are bits and pieces of information explaining how the concepts I have discussed apply to accountability. However, my goal from here forward is to discuss learning and how, if we coach our students in their endeavors to become readers, writers, and thinkers, they will all surely develop in these areas.

SUGGESTED READING

Brannon, Lil. (1983). The teacher as philosopher: The madness behind our method. *Journal of Advanced Composition, 4,* 25–32.

Conners, Robert J. (1981). The rise and fall of the modes of discourse. *College Composition and Communication, 32*(4), 444–455.

Fort, Keith. (1971). Form, authority, and the critical essay. *College English, 32*(6), 629–639.

Hairston, Maxine. (1982). The winds of change: Thomas Kuhn and the revolution in the teaching of writing. *College Composition and Communication, 33*(1), 76–88.

Knoblauch, C. H., & Brannon, Lil. (1997). *Rhetorical traditions and the teaching of writing.* Portsmouth, NH: Heinemann.

CHAPTER THREE

Coaching and Teaching by Doing

Modeling Thinking, Writing, and Reading

When I found that I was going to be coaching cross-country, I began to drag myself out to hit the pavement every day. It never occurred to me that I could coach runners without running myself. I never consciously thought about why my own ability to run would be important to my coaching; it was a natural assumption. One wouldn't take piano lessons from a person who did not play the piano.

So, when practice started, my athletes saw me sweating and suffering right along with them in the unbearable August heat. When they came by to ask a question during the school day, they saw me guzzling water just as I had instructed them to do in our constant effort to keep ourselves hydrated to avoid heat exhaustion.

When they asked me what to do when they felt winded, I could draw on my own experience from the day before to give them an answer. When we talked about running through "the wall," I knew exactly how they felt. When they lay like limp rags in the grass after a tough practice, I was right there with them, raglike myself. We all developed strength and speed throughout the season together. My athletes trusted my advice and instruction in part because they saw me following it every day.

That was my coaching life. My teaching life was much different.

A HORROR STORY IN TWO SCENES

Scene I: Sunday Night Back in the Dark Ages

I sit, staring at my plan book. It's Sunday night, and the week stretches out before me in nice, neat, little white blocks waiting to be filled with activities that will keep my students busy. I remember the words of my methods teacher: "Be sure to maintain a high time on task in your classroom." I remember my own high school teachers heaving a huge sigh, as if we were being granted some monumental favor, and saying, "We have a paper due tomorrow. If you are very quiet, you may write for the last 20 minutes of class." Then I remember the words of my principal: "The block schedule is not in place to allow students to begin their homework early. Use all 90 minutes for instruction."

I sigh. If I give students time to read and write in class, does that mean that I am wasting time that I should be using to *teach* them something? Surely they can read and write at home without me. But will they? I know often that the answer is no, especially for the ones who need to be reading and writing the most. Am I giving in to their laziness if I take class time for these activities, or is there another reason that the reading and writing never seems to happen at home? Should I be filling their heads with as much information about *how* to write as I can in 90 minutes and then send them home to actually do it? Should I be using that time to lecture about the novel we are reading so that I can make sure that they have the *right* interpretation?

Mercy! Can I even come up with 90 minutes worth of material to keep their attention? Certainly not! I'll put them into groups to get a discussion going. I'll give them some questions to guide their reading so that I can be sure that they are getting the *correct* information. Then we can share all of that information as a class.

There we go; that's a good plan. We'll hit the different learning styles; they can discover the answers to my questions on their own, then they can teach the information to each other under my watchful eye so that I can be sure that they are giving the *right* information. I've broken the period up so that they won't get bored, and I haven't wasted time letting them do things they could do at home. I'll tell them when the paper is due, and they can turn it in, with drafts of course, because I am a process writing teacher after all!

Whew, that was tough, but now I have plans for the week. I am a good teacher because I am not allowing them to waste time. Everything is instructional. I'll probably be teacher of the year soon.

Scene II: Sunday Night One Week Later

It's Sunday night again. I've written my plans for the following week, but I can't go to bed because I still have a stack of papers to grade. I've been putting it off all weekend. I read a couple Friday afternoon, and they were so awful that I just couldn't bring myself to read any more. Drafts are attached, but minus a few editing marks on some of them, they look suspiciously alike from first to last. How can this be—we've *talked* about revision!

The writing is boring, without life, and one paper is almost the same as the next. I'll absolutely die if I have to read what I said last Thursday one more time. I *told* them to use their own thoughts. Why do they keep doing this to me? AGRRR!!! I should have learned how to teach math.

*   *   *

When I was coaching, I felt a connection with what I was doing. In my classroom, there was an invisible wall. It was as though my students and I were fighting each other, pulling in opposite directions. They were pretty sure that I was trying to make their lives miserable, and I was pretty sure that they were trying to do the same to me.

Where was the connection to my students and their work? When I gave advice about writing and reading, it was purely academic. I was echoing the words of teachers before me. I had no gut reaction. I was not speaking from experience; I was simply preaching the same hollow words over and over again.

Enter a year off for graduate school, the National Writing Project, and the idea that teachers of writing should actually write. The co-leaders of the Summer Institute gave me permission to coach in my classroom. If we want students to become readers, writers, and thinkers, we must do it right along with them and then coach them through the rough spots, drawing from our own experience.

MODELING: A SIMPLE CONCEPT WITH HUGE BENEFITS

Modeling Gives Us Fresh Experiences to Draw From

Runners run. Carpenters work with wood. Painters paint, sculptors sculpt. Writers write and readers read. The most important thing that we can do for our students is to demonstrate our own writing and reading habits in order to help them form their own. Ellin Oliver Keene (Keene & Zimmermann, 1997) wrote, "For me and many other teachers I suspect, rediscovering our own subconscious processes of learning led to our most important progress in working with children" (p. 80). In order to teach writing and reading, we must first figure out how we do it ourselves. Regularly reading and writing with our students, and by doing that, modeling these processes for them over and over keeps the memory of what it is like to read and write fresh for us. When the students stumble, we have new experiences of our own to draw from. Our words of wisdom come directly from experience rather than from a text. When we don't read and write regularly, we quickly forget what it feels like to struggle with words, and our advice loses its validity.

Modeling Can Transform Our Classrooms

Modeling writing and reading for our students helps build community in the classroom. Tom Romano (1987) wrote:

> The sharing of my messes, my writing under construction, had a salutary effect on classroom atmosphere. I came to look upon my students differently. From a judge ready to pronounce a sentence I metamorphosed into an advocate of student writers, helper and fellow crafter. And their view of me changed. They began to perceive me as one who wrote and knew about writing, not merely as someone who was a stickler for standard usage and punctuation and who always had in mind an ideal way of writing something. The teacher, they saw, wrestled with the same problems they did—a comforting fact for a learner. (p. 40)

As students watch their teachers engage in the real act of writing or reading, they begin to trust us. As they trust, they learn that we are not trying to trick them into doing more work, and that we understand the struggles they go through when they write and read. Anyone who has ever spent very much time with teenagers knows the importance that being understood holds for them. Many aspects of my first year of teaching were magical. Looking back, I remember little about the trials of an inexperienced rookie. I do, however, remember the bond that I developed with those 119 eighth graders. I'm sure that some of that harks back to the fact that they were my first group of students; we went through the death of a classmate together, and they saw me with no makeup and in my PJs when we spent a weekend at the beach together. But I must also admit that by writing their first assignment, an experience paper, right along with them, I allowed them a deeply personal look at me as a human being. I became a real person who had a life outside of that classroom and made messes and struggled as she wrote. After that first assignment, I allowed myself to be convinced by other teachers that I didn't have time for such frivolity in my classroom. Now I look back on that year and sigh over the missed opportunity.

Modeling builds trust and community in the classroom not only because stories like Romano's support it, or because of the fact that when I saw those students in later years they would mention my propensity for throwing up on boats (my "experience" had been deep sea fishing), but because that class was different from the ones that followed it. For the reason I mentioned earlier, for the next two years I did not write with my students. I still enjoyed my students, and in most cases we eventually formed a bond, but the trust was much harder to come by. It took months to accomplish what I had accomplished in the first week that first year.

The year that I returned to teaching after graduate school held much of the same magic as that first year I taught. We had a bond! In the words of a brilliant colleague of mine, "We were a family." There is something very special that happens in a classroom when the teacher rolls up her sleeves and goes to work with the students.

When we ask our students to write or to discuss their true responses to literature, we are asking them to bare their souls. The difference between good and bad writing—and for that matter, good and bad reading—is the level at which the person opens up herself, her thoughts, and her feelings for others to see. A true image of any human being is often very flawed. As Romano (1987) points out, there is no time in life when it is more "agonizing" to be flawed than as a teenager. If we expect them to let us see their flaws, then we must show them ours as well. If we want honesty, we must give them honesty. Before we can get students to take risks, we must show them the rewards of such risks.

Modeling Fosters Authentic Learning

Community in our classrooms is important, but how will modeling really help students learn? In an interview I asked a student I was tutoring in the UNC-Charlotte Writing Center if he felt that modeling would help him write. I found quickly that the concept of watching a teacher write was not familiar to him. He also had some doubts about whether or not all students would benefit from it, especially those who just wanted to write and get it done, those who were not concerned about improving. But, he did feel that it would help those who truly wanted to learn. He even mentioned that he had begun to watch what "those people who are good" did and use the techniques they used in his own writing. Finding a model and learning from her was almost intuitive for this student.

Granted, the student I was interviewing was a very motivated student. He was at a point in his life when he wanted to learn to write because he saw it as a necessary skill for his future career. But imagine what could happen if the modeling was there for him in his class each day, if he didn't have to go out and seek it on his own? The possibilities are endless.

And what of those unmotivated students? Mike Rose, author of *Lives on the Boundary* (1989), was such a student, but once he found a model, he began to explode. His story is worth explaining because he is now an adult, which allows us to see the full results of this type of instruction without waiting 15 years to reinterview one's students. As a child, Mike had a full and wonderful imagination; he continually entertained the neighborhood children with stories of adventure. But in school he was immediately tracked into the lower-level courses. At an early age, it was decided that he and his classmates were not college material. School was a dull and boring world for him.

In high school, he was tracked into the Voc. Ed. program but had the good fortune of finding biology interesting. His teacher encouraged him to switch to the college track when he began to make 98s and 99s on his tests. And then he met Jack MacFarland. This young teacher *lived* to teach and talk about literature. Though Rose describes MacFarland's classroom as a rigorous one, the thing that kept this man's students coming to him after school when it wasn't required was the fact that he talked with them about literature and writing as if they were peers. He *showed* them how to talk about and love the written word. Mike was hooked.

With the help of Mr. MacFarland and his connections, Rose was accepted into a small private college at the end of his senior year. Things did not look good for him in college, until he had another breakthrough in his philosophy class. Mike's troubles were coming from the fact that he had never really learned how to think on his own. His philosophy teacher, Don Johnson, believed not only in the teaching of philosophy but the application of it. Mr. Johnson was studying to become a priest and was trying to form his own philosophies about life. He began to form these ideas in front of his students. In Mike's words, "He was working as a philosopher, and he was thinking out loud in front of us." Mike began to see what it really was to wrestle with a text and glean meaning from it (Rose, 1989, p. 49).

Today Mike Rose has a master's degree and works with remedial students at UCLA. He has written many books on the subjects that have inspired and instructed thousands of people. This unmotivated kid from the LA ghetto "got it." If you've ever read any of his work, you *know* he can write. Though there are many lessons in his story, one of the most powerful to me is that of modeling. When we model reading and writing for our students, we are really showing them how to think about and analyze language—their own as well as others. What the student in my interview did not see was that it is one of our many jobs as teachers to motivate our students, and modeling is a great way to do it. Truthfully, we can never be sure why our students are unmotivated to learn to write or read, but in my experience often the reason is pure and abject fear of the unknown and seemingly impossible. When we can dispel that fear, we can welcome these students into the mysterious fraternity of writers and lovers of language.

If we can break through the fear, then our students, like Mike Rose, will fly. A marvelous way to do so is to let our students see that writing and reading are messy processes that require discipline for everyone. Assigning writing and reading without showing students what writing and reading are really like is the real waste of time.

Modeling Will Supercharge Our Planning Time

Teachers work hard. I'd even dare to say that many of us wear our long hours as a badge of honor, and that's okay, coupled with commensurate results. As writing teachers, many of us struggle with giving our students time to write in class. We know that in our curriculum we must cover certain works of literature, grammar, and vocabulary as well as writing. As the war cry of "Accountability!" rises from the mouths of the masses, we do not have a single moment to waste. We want our students, their parents, and our colleagues to know that we are doing all we can to cover the material. But if we are teaching in the way I described as being the Dark Ages, then we are wasting our time as well as our students'. What if we were to spend even half of that planning time working on our own writing and reading? What if we dedicated class time not only to letting our students practice their reading and writing— a necessity that we discuss in the next chapter—but actually writing with them ourselves.

I did have a moment of clarity in the premodeling years; I just didn't know it at the time. About 2 weeks before I was to move from the middle school to the high school, the assistant principal, known for trying to nail young new teachers, walked into my classroom to do a surprise observation. "Teach something," she said when I explained that the students were going to be working on comparison papers that day. I had planned to let the students write in class because we had a short period that day, about 40 minutes, and I had found that these students were more likely to actually write the papers if I let them get started in class. I wasn't prepared to "teach" anything. *Big* trouble!

So, I pulled the overhead to the front of the room and started to plan a comparison paper in front of my students off the top of my head, in what I told the observers was to be a 15-minute mini-lesson. It was the most authentic writing experience my students had that year. They were mesmerized as I seemingly "pretended" to figure out what I wanted to compare. I made a list and then made a big mess on the overhead, drawing connections and writing notes in the margins as the ideas came to me. Though the students didn't realize it, they were seeing my real composing and thinking process right before their eyes as I connected the three pieces of literature we had been working with.

When I finished, the students immediately began making their own comparisons, and the assistant principal was ecstatic. I will never forget her words: "I have never seen someone teach comparison writing like that before. I was very skeptical at first, but the students really seem to have caught on. Excellent job." I breathed a sigh of relief, thinking nothing more than that I had done an excellent job faking it.

In many ways, truly modeling how we think and write about literature makes our planning time a little easier. Rather than spending hours planning how we will talk about a piece, it is sometimes better just to let the ideas flow so that the students can see our false starts and stops. The same applies for finding topics for students to write about in a piece of literature. I used to spend hours at home trying to come up with several concepts for students to write about so that they would have some choice. As I worked on my graduate degree, I began to see how much more valuable it is to let them watch me come up with my topic in class, and then let them choose their own as well. I can use all of that planning time to read the wonderful writing they are doing!

*   *   *

When I started coaching writing and reading the same way I coached running, my life became *much* simpler. Suddenly, I didn't have to know everything. I didn't have to plan hundreds of "activities" that the students would breeze through and learn little from. And more important, grading papers became a pleasure instead of a frustrating chore. Writing and reading with my students made my teaching more exciting, cut my planning time in half, *and* improved the quality of what was going on in my classroom a hundredfold. Time and curriculum were no longer at odds with one another. Everything we did in class became real and meaningful to all of us, my students as well as myself. The assessments and what the "powers that be" would think became background noise, while learning took the driver's seat.

MODELING IN OUR CLASSROOMS: WHAT DO WE *DO?*

Here I would like to offer a word of caution. Often when we think of modeling, we think in terms of offering skills to our students. We have a sort of "Here's what you need to do, now do it" mentality. This is not the type of modeling that I am talking about. Donald Graves (1996) says it best:

> Children select skills in modeling more easily because they are shown within the context of natural predicaments. Modeling can never be a substitute for the solution to children's own predicaments. It can however be a referral point for confirming what children themselves go through.
>
> The teacher does not use modeling to beat the child over the head with a new skill. Rather, the teacher uses the modeling to confirm the commonality of all writers, as well as to confirm new approaches by the child in the writing process. (p. 50).

We write with our students to give them a chance to observe a writer as he deals with real writing problems. By doing this, we offer our students a selection of skills to choose from, as they need them, while validating those problems as the difficulties that "real writers" have. The same goes for reading and thinking.

Because of the nature of modeling, I cannot provide lesson plans or activities. To model, I simply write, read, and think in front of my students. The best way for me to show modeling is to tell stories from my classroom.

Modeling Concepts for Writing

Mentors and Inspiration

I use published writers as my personal models for writing, and I have found it quite powerful for my students to see that fact. As I mentioned earlier, Donald Murray's *Shoptalk* (1990) is a great source of inspiration for me. Other great texts on writing include Anne Lamott's *Bird by Bird* (1994), Annie Dillard's *The Writing Life* (1989), and Stephen King's *On Writing* (2000). I place their quotes on the walls in my classroom. I refer to them often when I'm talking with my students about my writing as well as theirs. I also refer to them when I don't want to write or when I'm frustrated with what I am writing. In essence, I model first by showing students what can be learned from other writers. Though they see me as a professional, they see that I need direction and guidance just as they do.

Habit

One concept that changed my life as a writer and reinforced what I knew in my heart to be right for my students was that writers must cultivate a habit. Our students must develop a writing habit too. We cannot allow them to wait for inspiration or for some sainted muse. They need to write each day whether they feel like it or not, whether they have an idea or not, whether that writing is going well or not. Donald Murray (1990) has collected more than 130 quotes from published writers on the absolute necessity of developing a habit if one wishes to become a writer. For these people, writing sessions last anywhere from 30 minutes to 8 hours. They speak of their writing schedules like others might speak of an office job. The authors use phrases like "punching the clock" and "going to work," though the "going" usually means locking themselves in some retreat in their homes and working before dawn in their pajamas. People must write each day if they are to be writers. Guy de Maupassant sums up what it takes to be a writer: "Get black on white" (Murray, 1990, p. 58).

And so, students must see us write each day. I begin each class with 10 minutes of writing. I can take attendance within the first minute and spend the other 9 minutes writing. Students quickly learn that I value this time and that disruptions are not tolerated. Because *I* value the time, so do they, and by the second month of school interruptions are never an issue.

Discipline

Another important characteristic of the habits of writers is the discipline that they describe.

> *He should sit on his bottom in front of a table equipped with writing materials. If his top end fails him, at least his nether end won't.*
>
> —Aubrey Menen

I have to begin all over every day. I get up at 6 or 6:30 to clean the house, and feed the children, and cook our supper ahead of time, so that I can be perfectly free the instant the children leave for school; but then when they're gone I find I'd rather do almost anything than go into my study. The door is so tall and dark; it looms. The whole room smells like a carpenter's shop because of the wooden bookcases. Ordinarily, it's a pleasant smell, but mornings, it makes me feel sick. I have to walk in as if by accident, with my mind on something else. Otherwise, I'd never make it.

—Anne Tyler

Talent is cheap. What matters is discipline.

—André Dubus

I enjoy the process of writing. The torment comes in getting my bottom on the chair and in front of the typewriter.

—Caryl Rivers

These people are writers because they have the discipline to write. It is very difficult, often painful, for them to get started, but they know if they do, the words will eventually come. Beginning to write is like standing at the bottom of the hill I described in Chapter 1. The hardest part is putting one foot in front of the other and getting started. We often build momentum as we go, but if we never start, then we will never get anywhere. When I dread doing the writing I need to do, I refer to these quotes. I do the same for my students when they are facing the hill. We also spend time discussing the difficulties we face and celebrating the discipline we exercise in those cases.

Permission to Write Badly

A final concept that keeps me moving forward as a writer is that writers must give themselves permission to write badly if they are ever to get any writing accomplished. The goals that they set each day for themselves consist of numbers of words or pages, or hours spent writing. Not one of them said that they must write until they get something good. In fact, many spoke of not being able to tell good writing from bad when they first completed a day's work. What mattered was that they wrote *something*. They had faith that eventually the "something" would turn into something good.

> *I didn't express confidence so much as blind faith that if you go in and work every day it will get better. Three days will go by and you will think every day is terrible. But on the fourth day, if you do go in, if you don't go into town or out in the garden, something usually will break through.*
>
> —Joan Didion

> *It may be lousy stuff. But it is there, and I can make it better tomorrow. I have done something worthwhile with my day.*
>
> —Richard Marius

> *I set myself 600 words a day as minimum output, regardless of the weather, my state of mind or if I'm sick or well. There must be 600 finished words—not almost right words.*
>
> —Arthur Hailey

In order to be a writer, one must write each day with a set production goal in mind, without worrying about whether or not what is written is actually good. If we want our students to become writers, this is precisely the type of environment that we must create for them. We must *show* them how to have a habit and set goals based on quantity rather than quality at first. We must let them see our own bad writing and watch us keep at it until something breaks through, even if the breakthrough is in the form of a different topic altogether. We need to show them how the bad writing was necessary to get to the good stuff.

It makes no sense to preach process if we don't believe in it enough to do it ourselves and let our students *see* us do it!

Continuing to write each day when the writing isn't going well is painful. Students need to see us push through the pain in order to believe that not only is it normal, but necessary. My students and I refer to the quote wall often to keep each other going.

A Lesson in Modeling Writing

I found wonderful lessons during my first few weeks as a teacher. I found myself standing in front of an eighth grade English class that first year, and because I had always envisioned myself with seniors, I wasn't quite sure what to do with my prepubescent charges. I had read and studied Kirby's *Inside Out* (1981), and I decided that my students and I would kick off our year by writing about an experience. Based on a suggestion from *Inside Out*, I decided to write the first paper with them in order to show them how to pick a topic, get started, and revise. Looking back now, it's clear that there was much to be learned from the episode, misguided through it was. I tell it now so that others may benefit from my hindsight.

I came to class on the appointed day armed with three topics:

"Deep Sea Fishing"

"The First Time My Husband Proposed"

"My Wedding Day"

I wrote these on the overhead screen and began to briefly tell the students about each one. I'll let you see my words here because that actually was good modeling.

Deep Sea Fishing

When I was twelve I begged my daddy to let me go deep sea fishing with him and my brother. I had to promise to act like a boy and that included not complaining if I got sick. The day turned out to be a stormy one, and though the captain offered to turn the boat around and take us home, my father insisted that we could handle it if the boat could. I threw up all day and that was the last time I went deep sea fishing.

The First Time My Husband Proposed

My husband and I both went to school at UNC–Chapel Hill. When we had been dating about 5 months, we went to a party at his fraternity house. Things started to get a little nuts after a while and we went up on the roof to take a breather. While we were standing up there looking at the lights on Franklin Street, he turned to me in a very matter of fact manner and said, "Some day I'm going to marry you." I didn't seem to have a choice in the matter at all.

My Wedding Day

I was married on March 30, 1996. My in-laws chartered a bus to bring all of their friends down South for the big event. It was a cloudy, cool day, but a beautiful ceremony and everyone had lots of fun at the two receptions. My feet were black and blue the following morning from dancing the polka all night long.

After listening to all of these stories about their teacher's life, my students were hooked into the activity. For about 5 minutes I fielded questions on the topics, and then I let them vote on which one I should write. Among my five classes, there was a tie between "The First Time My Husband Proposed" and "Deep Sea Fishing." When I returned the next day, I told them that I had chosen "Deep Sea Fishing" because even though I liked the other stories, I thought I had the most vivid memories of the fishing trip.

I then asked my students to come up with three topics of their own and allowed them to discuss them in small groups. Because we had already had such a discussion as a whole group, they knew what to do. Each student told a little about their stories; the group questioned the student and suggested a topic; and then the student picked a topic based on what she thought she knew the most about, based on the conversations they had just had. Overall, I felt like the activity was successful. There were some students who had difficulty coming up with topics at first, but as they talked together in groups, one student's idea sparked something in another, and they all eventually found something that they could write about. "Okay," I thought. "This is working."

A big problem for students is getting started once they have chosen a topic. I thought that I was modeling getting started with my eighth graders by using the fishing story. The night before I planned to have them free write (called a "zero draft" at that point in my career) I sat down and wrote for about 50 minutes about my fishing trip. I didn't correct spelling or grammar, and I didn't really worry about organization. I just wrote as the thoughts came to me. I edited out the complete nonsense where I was talking to myself, and I made transparencies for class discussion the next day.

After my students got over the shock of seeing such a mess in a teacher's writing, they started to make suggestions. They wanted to immediately correct all my spelling and grammar, but they didn't have much to say about the content of the piece except, "That's really good." I began to ask them questions and move ideas around on the screen. We spent about 20 minutes reorganizing the piece, and then I asked them to tell me what they wanted to know more about. They were full of ideas. I wrote their suggestions in the margins of my piece as they talked and explained that I would work on it and bring it back the next day. Satisfied that they knew what to do, I told them to get started on their own pieces. I reminded them that this was the zero draft, so all I wanted them to do was get their ideas down on paper. I was feeling pretty successful. This writing stuff was a piece of cake!

About half of my students did just as I expected. They dove right in and began to write furiously about their chosen topic. But the other half just sat and stared at the blank page. I was baffled. As I sat and worked with them, I found that they just did not know how to begin. "But you just *watched* me get started," I said. "What don't you understand?" One of the more outspoken people in the group said, "But you're an *English* teacher, and you wrote 10 pages! We can't do that; we're only in the eighth grade! It's just not the same." I made a note in my journal that day that this modeling stuff was turning into a waste of time.

I realize now that I skipped a step in my modeling. I should have written that zero draft in front of my students. They needed to see me sitting and thinking. They needed to see the "talking to myself" parts that I had edited out. They needed to see me searching for words and attempting to find that first line that usually gets me started. They needed to see me struggle. Seeing the imperfect results of that struggle simply was not enough. To them, my imperfect results were much better than anything they felt capable of in a first draft, and though I knew that I was far from finished, the paper that I brought to them did not dispel the myth of what my students considered brilliant thoughts coming easily.

*   *   *

I'll share a much more successful venture in modeling next. The year after I finished graduate school, my standard-level tenth graders and I were working through a poetry unit. We were trying to write our own sonnets, *trying* being the operative word. Poetry has never been my strong suit, and the sonnet is a difficult form. We all sat, struggling to make our thoughts fit the form. I could hear the sighs of frustration all around me. I looked up from my own mess just in time to see three heads go down. Looking back down, I felt as frustrated as they did. My teaching in that moment consisted of one simple phrase: "I don't know about you all, but I'm really having a hard time with this. Want to hear what I have so far?"

After we all stopped laughing at my pitiful attempt, we went back to work with renewed vigor. Seeing me struggle, knowing that it wasn't simply a performance for their benefit helped them remember that this is what writing is all about. We had this experience on May 3, nearly the end of the school year. The concept needed to be driven home over and over again. Modeling once in the beginning of the year just doesn't cut it.

*   *   *

When I thought that I was modeling free writing for eighth graders, I was actually modeling revision. Since then I have found that modeling is the *only* way to truly teach revision. Students have difficulty with revision for many of the same reasons that they have difficulty getting started. They don't want to let go of any of the words that they manage to write, and they don't want to recopy their papers. In many ways, we as teachers are responsible for this attitude. The lesson plan I wrote about at the beginning of this chapter is an example of how we have fostered it. Not only have we not shown the students how to revise, but we haven't given them time to do it in class. According to Janet Emig (1983), students perceive such behavior to mean that only the final product is important. She then points to the practice of allowing students to "revise for a better grade." I thought that I was being a wonderful teacher when I allowed students such a second chance. I thought I was modeling the writing process, seeing my students' writing as a work in progress, and allowing them to continue working on it with the benefit of my comments. According to Emig's study, as well as the looks on my students' faces when I told them that they needed to revise to raise the F's I had marked on their papers, my students translated my actions into the idea that "people do revision when they do not do a good job the first time" (p. 83).

Oh, how our well-intentioned actions change meaning in the minds of our students! Not only have the practices just described warped our students' perceptions of what we mean when we talk about revision, they have also confused them about the nature of writing in general. It's no wonder those students from my first year were still having trouble getting started with their writing even after looking at my draft. If revision were a punishment for doing something wrong, then in order to be a "good" writer, every word a person wrote would have to be golden.

I *began* modeling revision for my eighth graders when I put my draft on the overhead to show them what a mess it was. As I asked them questions, answered their questions, and wrote in the margins, they began to get a taste of what revision was. They could begin to see what kinds of questions they needed to ask of themselves and of each other as they revised their own work. As one of them so aptly put it later, "Revision is making a big mess of your paper and then straightening it out again." Still, showing them that first step wasn't enough. I did go home and revise the piece based on our discussion, and they were quite amazed at how very different it looked. I distinctly remember the pained expression on one student's face as he shook his head and said, "It's completely different; you just started over. You wrote all those other pages for nothing." He felt sorry for me. In his mind, I had just messed up the first time. He would need to see me go through this process over and over before he ever figured out that this was the way my writing always looked in the beginning. One of the hardest concepts for students to grasp or accept about writing is the time that it takes to make something good.

Not only did I need to let my students watch me write, but also I needed to do it often. That first year I was operating under the assumption that Donald Graves (1996) warned us about. I was planning to model a skill and expecting my students to understand the concept and apply it to their own writing immediately. Because I was thinking in terms of specific skills, I skipped important steps in writing that I wasn't even aware existed. Some of my students were going to need to watch me write for most of the year before the concepts I was showing them about how to get started and how to revise ever came to them. They needed to reach that point in their own writing before they would come to see how it would work for them. Others needed to be convinced that the concepts I was using actually worked. They would not believe in them until they saw them produce better writing for me as well as for their classmates over and over again.

*   *   *

Modeling is not a quick fix. But then, as you will remember from Chapter 2, the quest for the quick fix is what produced false systems that were hurtful rather than helpful to our young writers. It is not enough to show students a finished product as a model. That's simply offering them a frame in which to force their own thoughts. Show them varieties of finished products, or none at all, and then model how to get there.

Modeling Concepts for Reading

Proficient Reader Strategies

In the same way, we need to teach students to read based on what real readers do. When I first began to think about the concept of real readers, I was thinking about literary critics as a source. Somehow, that didn't seem right. I know plenty of people whom I would consider real readers who have never written criticism. Then some colleagues of mine in the UNC–Charlotte Writing Project introduced me to a book called *Mosaic of Thought* (Keene & Zimmermann, 1997). My friends, Diane Wildeman and Karen Haag, were involved in an interesting project. Diane was a high school English teacher and Karen was an elementary literacy specialist. Diane invited Karen to the high school to help her work with struggling readers. The outcome was amazing. As these women were presenting their project in a summer seminar, they discussed the importance of the "proficient reader" strategies found in *Mosaic of Thought*. The strategies are based on the belief that

> proficient readers know what and when they are comprehending; they can identify their purposes for reading and identify when and why the meaning of the text is unclear to them, and use a variety of strategies to solve comprehension problems or deepen their understand of a text. (Keene & Zimmerman, 1997, p. 22)

> Proficient readers

> - activate prior knowledge in order to better understand and remember a text;
> - determine what are the most important ideas and use that conclusion to focus their reading;
> - ask questions of the text, the author, and themselves as they read in order to clarify and focus their reading;
> - create pictures in their minds as they read in order to clarify and remember text;
> - draw inferences from the text by using prior knowledge and experiences to predict what will happen, draw conclusions, or come up with new ideas;
> - synthesize a text to understand what they have read;
> - use fix-up strategies to help them when comprehension breaks down. (Keene & Zimmerman, 1997)

For me, *proficient readers* translates as "real readers." The message I took from Diane and Karen's research is, if we expect our high school students to be proficient readers, we must continually model these strategies for them. It is incorrect to believe that our students know how to read carefully from their elementary education. Some may have learned these strategies, but many may not have. Also, there is something strange that happens when students enter high school. The course we teach changes from language arts to English, and for many students, it becomes something completely different. Students of all academic levels need to be reminded of these strategies, and we all know of the low retention rate of lectures. Students need to *see* these things happening for us as we read with them.

But, as with writing, we must be careful to not simply model the list point by point and then expect students to apply it. We must go through the process of thinking about what we read in front of them. These strategies are a great beginning for our struggling readers, and great reminders for our more advanced students when they find themselves faced with challenging texts.

Literary Analysis

As our students grow as readers, we expect their understanding of the works they read to deepen dramatically, but we must remind them that they still begin from the same place they always have, figuring out what the text is about and reacting to that. The best way to do that is by modeling for them.

There is much more to teaching literature at the high school level than simply having students answer comprehension questions and then testing them on literary terms, and it is certainly more than lecturing on themes we have previously identified. Teaching literature involves coaching students through how to "think" about what they read.

Modeling reading and literary study is much more than reading out loud to students. I've often read out loud to my students. Sometimes I read to the students just to get them hooked into a piece, and other times I read entire novels to them, especially in my lower-level classes. I would stop, and they would answer tons of comprehensions questions on each chapter. I would lecture to them about themes from the copious notes I had taken on my interpretation of the work the night before. (I called it a discussion, but usually I was doing all of the talking and they were taking notes.) I prided myself on asking test questions that required higher-order thinking skills, but in reality, I was the one doing all of the thinking. All the students had to do was memorize what I had said to them in class and then give it back to me on the test.

By the end of each term, most of my students knew the stories we had covered, but they were no closer to being able to read and comprehend those texts on their own, or even wanting to for that matter, than the day they first walked into my classroom. When

I began to model some of the thinking I was doing, let them see me struggle with my interpretations, let them see proficient reader strategies, let them watch me think out loud, they began truly to learn to think for themselves.

The important difference between my thinking and the students' is that I am more experienced in thinking about literature, so I can give our discussion a direction that otherwise would not be there. I know what we should be thinking about. And that's what we want to teach them, *how* to go about working with and interpreting a piece of literature, not *what* to think. Many of our students suffer under the illusion that as English teachers we know all there is to know about everything we read as soon as we read it. They don't realize that we have read it a dozen times and that we come up with new ideas each time we read it. Or even worse, they assume that we are just using the materials from the teacher's manual. That certainly isn't modeling learning to think for oneself!

A Lesson in Modeling Close Reading and Analysis

When I went back to work after graduate school, I had the good fortune to be assigned to the Tenth Grade International Baccalaureate (IB) English students. At first I was worried that I would not be able to continue my research with such high-functioning children. *Boy,* was I wrong.

Through a series of events, I found that I needed to begin the year with an African novel. I had always wanted to explore Chinua Achebe's novel *Things Fall Apart* (1959), and now seemed the perfect time.

So, I read the novel. "Hmmm!" was really all of the first impression that I had. I was *not* impressed, but school was starting and I didn't have time to find another African novel. I noticed that after I got through Part I of *Things Fall Apart* the story picked up. I decided, and told my students, that we must suffer through Part I in order to understand the culture that was so very different from our own. Luckily, by this point I had realized that I didn't have to know everything about a piece of literature before I began teaching it. I figured that *Things Fall Apart* would be a true test of what I had come to discover in graduate school. We would have to discover what it was about together. "No chance of me lecturing too much with this one," I thought. "I really don't have that much to say."

That attitude caused me no small amount of panic that first day as I looked into the faces of those extremely intelligent students, pencils poised, ready to write down all of the wisdom that I uttered. I didn't really have that much for them in terms of the novel. I gulped and plunged forward, silently wondering if maybe I hadn't made a big mistake by not starting with *Oedipus*, something I'd taught about a hundred times.

The experience was wonderful. Each literature day we would begin with a little response writing to get our brains clicking; mine included, I was rereading right along with them. Then, in my master plan I had a little time scheduled for some class discussion before they broke into literature groups to work through some things that I wanted them to think about. These discussions were some of the richest I had ever experienced. In the beginning I wondered if it was simply because I was working with such intelligent students, but later as I worked through literature that I knew more about, I discovered that they were rich because I didn't have all of the answers and I really didn't have an agenda. Since then I have learned to begin all discussions by asking if there are any questions about the reading. As soon as my students become comfortable with questioning as a proficient reader strategy rather than as a sign of not knowing the answer, they always have a list ready for such opportunities. Then, I let the students answer each other's questions, with my comments only sparsely woven in as I discover new things about the text because of what they are saying. No matter what, I resist the urge to respond with a lecture.

Typically, a discussion goes like this:

Urbanski: So before we split into groups, are there any questions?

A tentative hand goes into the air.

Student 1:   Why in the world did that medicine man dig up a rock after following that child all over the tribe's lands?

Urbanski: That's a good question, anyone have any ideas about that?

A long pause as they all tried to wait me out—it was going to be a long wait, because I didn't really have an answer.

Student 2:   Well, in the book they said they were trying to keep her from dying.

Student 3:   Yeah, wasn't it something about the mother—however you say her name—had had a bunch of miscarriages and was really worried that her one living child would die?

Student 1:   Yeah, but how was digging up a rock going to stop that from happening? These people are so *dumb.*

Student 3:   Hey wait a minute, maybe you're dumb! Who's to say witch doctors aren't real?!

Urbanski: All right, settle down, nobody's dumb, remember our rule about no cheap shots. The two of you take a breather for a few minutes and collect yourselves. Something you all just said made me think of something I hadn't before, what about the placebo drugs our medical science uses, could this maybe be related to that?

(I wasn't pretending, I had really just thought of that.)

Student 2:   Hey! That makes sense. Maybe the witch doctor's power is really over their minds!

Student 4:   Yeah, but why wouldn't he have dug up the rock when she was a baby, and how does he know she's not going to die and expose him as a big fraud?

Student 5:   If he had dug it up when she was a baby, then the chance of her dying would have been much greater—didn't the book say she was sick a lot?

Pages start flipping as a couple of students as well as myself start hunting through the novel for that information.

Student 6:   Maybe he can tell that she's strong enough to make it now—that she's just got a cold—nothing that will kill her.

Student 1:   Yeah, but how does he know she won't die?

Urbanski: Well, if she does get sick and die later, what's to stop him from saying it was because of something else—maybe since she has reached this age the people would believe that she was too old to be an *ochi* anymore.

At this point in the discussion we are all looking around the room at each other, quite pleased with ourselves for unraveling such a complex novel. Suddenly, many parts of it are making more sense to me, and from the look on my students' faces, I can see the same thing happening to them. Part I was much more interesting and important than we had originally thought. I have to restrain myself from going into a lecture that is forming in my mind about Achebe's attitude toward the Ibo culture, how he feels about the people he is writing about, how the novel would be different if his tone were different. I have to cover my mouth with my hands from blurting out all of the things I am suddenly seeing as pivotal to the novel and Achebe's purpose in writing it that exist in Part I. Instead, I force myself to simply ask a question:

Urbanski: So, why do you think this is in here? Let's all take 2 minutes to write about this.

I wildly start to scribble down all of my new thoughts so that I don't forget them. Most of the students do the same, while others look around the room, then slowly pick up their pens. They will need to see this process a few more times in order to be convinced of its purpose.

After the writing time, the students decide that it's time to begin working in their literature circles because this is "a toughie."

As I wander from group to group, I find my students engaged in a wonderful discussion on *tone* and its importance to a novel without actually using the word. I let them work for about 15 minutes before writing the word in big, bold letters on the board. I don't say anything. I simply let the word stand and watch it pick up like wildfire.

Student 1:   What's that up there for?

Student 2:   I don't know, maybe we're going to talk about that later?

Student 3:   Mrs. U., is that going to be on the test?

Student 4:   What's tone?

Urbanski: I'm not telling, it's just a little hint.

Student 4:   Dang it, she never tells us anything, do you know what tone is?

Student 3:   Yeah, we talked about it last year, but I don't really remember.

Student 2:   Look it up in the back of one of those lit books, they always have definitions.

Student 3:   Okay, the author's attitude toward his subject matter.

Student 1:   What's that got to do with anything?

Student 4:   I don't know, I hate literary terms; I was having more fun talking about the witch doctor stuff; why do teachers always have to ruin everything?

Student 1:   Wait, there has to be a reason for this. Hey! That is what we are talking about—she said, "Why is this in here?" Achebe talks about witch doctoring like it really is something, he has a good attitude about the Ibo, that's his *tone!*

Student 2:   Hey Mrs. U, come over her, I think we've got it!

And they circle and circle and talk and talk until they all finally understand tone and can apply it to *Things Fall Apart*. Now, this took an entire 90-minute class period. I realize that I could have lectured on Achebe's use of tone in about 15 minutes. I also realize that I could have put them into cooperative groups and given them some very leading questions to be sure that they figured out tone, and that would have taken about 30 minutes. The difference is threefold:

1. I didn't know I would be teaching tone that day. I knew it was something that they needed to learn, and it was what came out of our discussion and my modeling how one thinks about literature with the question, "Why is this in here?"

2. The students had ownership of the term rather than a vocabulary lesson.

3. They learned much more than the word *tone*. They saw me thinking right along with them, though I had to convince them that I really was right there with them because IB students are somewhat jaded and firmly believe in the power of their teachers to manipulate their minds and pretend (much like a witch doctor).

It was tough for my students to believe that I didn't know all the answers and was depending on them to help me think, and even tougher for me to admit it. In the end they came to trust me, and our discussions grew richer with each piece of literature we tackled. By the time we reached works I was really familiar with, we were all so comfortable with real discussion that it was almost impossible for me to revert back into lecturing and content questions. The students simply had too much to say.

CONCLUSIONS: PULLING IT ALL TOGETHER AND COMING FULL CIRCLE

How very different my classroom became after I began modeling reading, writing, and thinking for my students consistently. I noted at the end of that year how very different my life had become. It was almost as if a different woman were writing the lesson plans. And a different person was—I was a coach now, not a lecturer.

One of our last tasks for the year (excluding our portfolios, of course) was to write an essay about a piece of literature we'd read that year. After a year of the students watching me come up with my own topics and in turn coming up with their own, I was delighted with the topics my tenth graders chose for their final literature piece. Even after the state writing test, for which they were asked to write from a specific (if not very limited) topic, most students were not only able to come up with something interesting to write about, but they were excited about it. I know that as I read the essays, I had to remind myself that these students were 15 years old.

And grading was such a treat. Instead of sitting down to read 70 papers that were identical, I was able to read 70 papers that were carefully crafted and very different in subject matter and style. Look at Jacob's opening:

Many works of literature contain a tragic hero, a character who has a final revelation before coming to a tragic end. Frequently, a tragic hero is the main character, such as Okonkwo in *Things Fall Apart* by Chinua Achebe. Another case is when the tragic hero is not the main character, which often leaves their revelations underdeveloped or unrealized by the reader. Such an example is Javert from *Les Miserables* by Victor Hugo. Still other authors choose to try to explain the thought process of these unfortunate characters, notable among them is George Orwell in his novel *1984* and Fyodor Dostoyevsky in *Crime and Punishment.*

To first begin to understand what a tragic hero is, and more importantly, how the tragic hero thinks and how the tragic hero archetype is often times a reflection of human society and human consciousness, one must first examine several of these characters to find their similarities. Tragic heroes have been used in literature throughout different times and cultures, demonstrating the universal appeal and importance of their inner character. The four novels dealing with tragic heroes discussed in this essay span a variety of times and cultures: *Things Fall Apart* set in early colonial Nigeria, *Crime and Punishment* in Tsarist Russia, *Les Miserables* in post-Napoleonic France, and *1984* written in 1949 as a warning to people about government's increasing influence in their lives. Each novel brings separate political, cultural, and social issues to the table, but each in some way or another focuses on the composition and motives of a tragic hero.

The wonderful thing about Jacob's paper is that he reached beyond the work we had read and discussed in class. After watching me model interpretation and practicing his own (as we discuss in the following chapter), he was ready to branch out. Confidence is what allows our students to become real readers and writers. I'll never forget the pride on his face as he turned in his extremely well-written and well-thought-out 10-page essay.

Elisha's paper is wonderful for its succinct and masterful dealing with a topic we touched upon ever so briefly in class. He dove in and worked with it on his own. A glance at his opening paragraph hooks the reader:

Victor Hugo's *Les Miserables* should be commended for its promotion of rebellion, love, pursuit of justice, and other such principles that are essential to mankind. It is unfortunate, however, that Hugo could not accomplish this without demeaning the women in his novel. He obviously has the misconstrued belief that women are in some way inferior to men; that they are incapable of important tasks, and that they tend to degenerate. I would very much like to rave about this novel, but the male chauvinism is a scar that cannot be overlooked.

Elisha took his topic from a discussion we had in class that was started by a student asking if we thought Hugo hated women. I had never thought about his treatment of women in the novel, so again, I was thinking out loud right along with them as we discussed her questions. Elisha's paper went far beyond our discussion and showed his ability to think about literature for himself.

In order to grow as readers, writers, and thinkers, our students need to watch us do precisely that. They need to see an adult go through the whole process: the trials and tribulations of getting started, throwing material out, adding new material, crossing out words, making a mess. When we are modeling, we are not teaching mini-lessons in these areas and then requiring students to do the same thing in order to prove that they know how. We are simply writing, reading, and thinking in front of them, so that when they go to read, write, and think themselves, they will have an arsenal from which to choose when they encounter authentic problems. When writing about writing with his students, Tom Romano (1987) states, "I removed the last vestige of mystery from writing. Truth replaced hocus-pocus" (p. 41). How powerful!

If we mean to teach students to write, read, write about what they are reading, and think about what they are reading and writing, we must do it with them. We must meet them on the academic playing field and sweat it out with them each and every day. We can't be afraid of making mistakes or not knowing the answer, because these are the true teachable moments in our classrooms. It's the humanity of the teacher-coach that gives the student the confidence to trust, and then, take a risk and learn.

CHAPTER FOUR

Warming Up the Writing Muscles

Two Tools for Invention

The biggest challenge any writer faces is coming up with an idea. I often find that my students would much prefer that I give them a topic to write about than choose their own, because it allows them to skip the invention process altogether. Still, their writing is far more insightful when it is based in a topic they created themselves or at least in ideas that they have found on their own. How can students ever come to see themselves as writers if they never choose what they write about? Without that choice, they are simply drones handing in work to the queen bee teacher. Two tools that I find invaluable for invention are free writing and the daybook.

FREE WRITING

"I just don't know where to start; I don't know what I want to say about this." Mike, a student at the UNC-Charlotte Writing Center, sat with his 6-foot-7 frame crammed into the suddenly tiny writing center chair, looking dejectedly at the blank computer screen. "Well, how about writing about it?" I responded. Wanting to please me, Mike placed his huge hands on the keyboard and began to type. Before he could begin composing, he had to head the

53

paper with his own name, the course number, and his teacher's name in bold and set the font and format of the page. Finally, he took a deep breath and rapidly typed out a sentence. He paused to read back over it and then started to fix all of the red and green lines placed there by Word to mark errors. He read the sentence again and inserted a few words here and there. Finally somewhat satisfied, he moved to the next sentence and repeated the same process. Eventually, Mike came up with one paragraph that would eventually turn into a one-page proposal. Then, before we could work with that paragraph, he had to spell check it.

In my conference log I noted two things about this session:

1. Didn't understand his issue

2. Didn't understand assignment

Reading further through my notes, I noticed something else: The writing Mike did in our session had done nothing to improve his understanding of either his issue or the assignment. He censored every word and syllable that came through his fingers and onto the computer screen. He was unable to focus his thoughts on what he was trying to say because he was too busy worrying about correctness. His own self-editing was slowing him down. There was a question here: How do we get kids to experience the magic of discovery, the flight, the running that is available to them through free writing?

What Is Free Writing . . . Really?

Free writing is a term that has been bantered about since the 1970s. Mike even referred to free writing in a conversation we had about his high school days. But though many of us have heard the term, there seem to be some discrepancies about what it actually means. Mike thought that he was free writing for me in the session I just described, but I saw nothing "freeing" about the process he was going through. He was constantly self-editing and referring back to the text and the computer. He could not possibly think about what he had written until he had corrected all of the spelling and grammar mistakes noted by the computer.

My view of free writing is writing at such a rate of speed that the voice in my head takes over and starts to express itself through my fingers. If I were to stop to check the squiggles on the screen or to be sure that I spelled something correctly, I would lose my train of thought. The voice that begins to speak in free writing seems completely independent from the rest of my brain. I feel like I am taking dictation. Other, more well-known writers feel the same way:

> *I don't feel that I wrote these books, I feel as though they had been written by my arm, by my brain, my organism, but that they're not necessarily mine.*
>
> —Paul Bowles

> *Creativity is continual surprise.*
>
> —Ray Bradbury

> *No surprise for the writer, no surprise for the reader. For me the initial delight is in the surprise of remembering something I didn't know I knew.*
>
> —Robert Frost

From these few examples we can see how professional writers describe the feeling of being carried away by their work. As a teacher of writing, I want my students to experience the feeling these authors had. Other teachers who write about writing have come up with many different terms for the practice of writing without stopping. Ken Macrorie and Peter Elbow coined the phrase "free writing," and Donald Murray (1999) has referred to it as "following a line of language." My favorite is Tom Romano's (1987) term, "cutting loose." "Teachers must cut [students] loose on the first day. Let them write in any form they choose. But make sure they write and sustain that writing long enough to rev up their voices" (p. 7). Let them go, let them fly. Let them run.

Why Does Free Writing Work?

In my first few years of teaching, I had encountered quite a bit of resistance to having students free write because many of my colleagues considered it a waste of time. I decided that if I were going to use free writing regularly in my classroom, I needed to find out more about it.

I found countless resources on the importance of free writing in process writing classrooms. Tom Romano (1987) bases his entire first chapter on the topic. In *Write to Learn* (1999), Donald Murray touts the practice over and over again. The first chapter of Peter Elbow's *Writing Without Teachers* (1973) is entitled "Free Writing Exercises." The list goes on. I found that I was in good company with my ideas of free writing; not only did I have the support of writers, but of teachers of writing as well. Still, I wondered *why* it worked.

To truly answer this question, one would have to do a study of the inner workings of the human mind. Here I will touch upon some of the theory that informs the practice of free writing. Epistemic rhetoricians view writing as a way to make knowledge. Put simply, writing helps us figure things out. Lil Brannon is one example of such a theorist. In her article entitled, "Teacher as Philosopher: The Madness Behind Our Method" (1983), she explains that writing is "a way of composing, a way of discovering connections among bits and pieces of experience and rendering it coherent" (p. 28). Writing is discovering what there is to say; it is the making of meaning out of the jumbled thoughts of the mind. She goes on to describe the true meaning behind the phrase "writing process" in terms of modern rhetoric: "[It] is not a procedure. Rather the term is used to describe the complex mental acts of forming ideas from the chaos of the experience and the connection of these ideas one statement at a time" (p. 29). Her use of the term *chaos* echoes the words of the writers we discussed earlier. Writing, and therefore free writing, works because it helps us put those jumbled thoughts down in the manner in which they come, so that we can go back later and refine them.

In his description of writing and thinking, Peter Elbow (1973) claims:

> Meaning is not what you start out with but what you end up with. . . .
>
> Writing is a way to end up thinking something you couldn't have started out thinking. Writing is, in fact, a transaction with words whereby you *free* yourself from what you

presently think, feel, and perceive. You make available to yourself something better than what you'd be stuck with if you'd actually succeeded in making your meaning clear at the start. (p. 15)

Elbow feels that free writing "frees" us from preconceived notions that may have clogged our thinking. We make meaning in writing simply by the fact that we write without worrying about the meaning. In this way we open ourselves up to those ideas that we have ignored or locked away.

Finally, I thought about an essay by John Locke titled "An Essay Concerning Human Understanding" (1690/1997). "Of Words," the third chapter of the essay, describes the human's use of language. Locke states that words are symbols of human thought. They are the mechanism by which we transfer our thoughts to others. He goes on to say that our concepts of words are colored by our experience. He uses the example of the word *gold* to illustrate this idea. A child just introduced to the word *gold* may use it to describe everything of that color. A more experienced child will find that gold is also shiny.

Following Locke's line of reasoning, when we free write we are able to put words on paper that represent our thoughts, though imperfectly. After we have these recorded, we can go back and worry about the business of accuracy. Free writing lets us make meaning first at a very elementary level by using words that represent our thoughts to us without worrying about the understanding of someone else.

Free writing works because we can use language in order to tame the chaos in our minds created by all of the thoughts produced by experiences. When we let those thoughts come freely and then represent them on paper in a way that only we need understand, we open the floodgates for all of the ideas that the magnificent human brain contains.

Application: Helping Our Students Discover the Magic

I wanted to study free writing in an environment where I was not responsible for making assignments, grading them, or teaching literature before I tried it in a setting where I had to do all three. My attitude about the usefulness of free writing was decidedly strengthened by the study experience, and I hope reading about it will do the same for you.

I sat out to work with and study three very different students and the way they were affected by using free writing. (All students' names have been changed in order to protect their privacy.) I selected Anson, Mike, and Tamara because I worked with them on a regular basis in the UNC-Charlotte Writing Resources Center, and because I felt them to be fairly representative of the different populations one might encounter in a high school classroom. Over the course of a semester, they all came to me with different attitudes, had different experiences, and experienced different outcomes using the free writing technique.

There was much to be learned from these students, and though my work with them was in a very different setting than what we experience at the high school level, I have found the lessons these students taught to be quite applicable to our high school classrooms. Over the years free writing has been one of the most valuable tools I have given to any student. Still, it takes a bit of convincing in the beginning, and I always have to remind myself of the premises that the three students in the writing center taught me and convince new students of them as well.

1. Mistakes are permissible and expected.

2. Free writing *is* efficient.

3. False starts happen (and sometimes lead to good starts).

4. It takes *time* to make magic.

Let's take a moment here to unpack these ideas.

Mistakes Are Permissible and Expected

According to my students, it's important to reassure them at the beginning that mistakes of writing etiquette are okay in the free writing phase. It is perfectly acceptable to digress, misspell words, talk to yourself, and deviate from standard English. This is a difficult concept for them to grasp at first, but without it, they will never feel their thoughts take over. If a student is trying to remember comma rules while writing down his ideas, he will most likely lose the thread of what they he was trying to say. Comma rules are important—but only after the ideas are on the paper.

Free Writing Is Efficient

We must convince students that generating ideas before trying to write the actual paper is truly more efficient than hammering away at perfect phrases one at a time if the goal is to create good writing. Too often our students are looking for the quickest way to get the writing done rather than the best way. In a reflection written to his professor about a college-level expository writing course a student wrote:

> When I write, all I concentrate on is getting to the point and getting the hell out of there. I found out quickly that this was not going to cut it in your class. Since the first assignment, I feel so much more comfortable with my writing. I don't freak out or stress about writing now, I just simply do it with no worries. With each assignment I find myself being a little more creative and freer with my words. This comes as a great surprise to me because I thought I would never be comfortable with my words.

We too must let our students know that "getting to the point and getting the hell out" is not acceptable. We expect and want much more from our students. We want them to feel and experience the magic and liberation of free writing. This student has learned that by taking the time to explore his thoughts, he not only can create "good" writing, but he can also become comfortable with it.

False Starts Happen (and Sometimes Lead to Good Starts)

Along with knowing that a person needs time to generate ideas that work, we need to let our students know that sometimes the ideas don't work, and that's okay too. Tamara was not afraid to admit that the "University Goals" paper was not going anywhere for her, so she changed ideas. Professional writer Ann Beattie puts Tamara's actions into words: "If I get to page three or four and the material hasn't shown me the way, I don't revise, I throw it out" (Murray, 1990, p. 96).

Not letting go of an idea that wasn't going anywhere was a big obstacle for Mike. Once he had used the quote that he later turned into a claim in his proposal paper, he had a very hard time letting go of it for the next paper, even when he could tell that it was not working for him.

It Takes Time to Make Magic

We must also encourage students to try free writing, and then try it again until they relax, see their own potential, and find their way. Much of what I have said here will mean nothing to students until they actually begin to free write. Then, we need to be there to coach them through the rough spots, to remind them of all we have said about free writing from the beginning. We cannot allow them to quit before they get over the hump. Anson was resistant to free writing in the beginning, but as he began to see that he was going to have to try something if he ever wanted to write without coming to the writing center, he decided to go for it. Free writing eventually became an integral part of his writing process. He used it more and more, and it worked for him more and more. I highly doubt that he will ever attempt to write anything of consequence again without free writing.

"But does it work that well with younger students?" you may be asking. Take a look at what this 15-year-old had to say:

> My freewrites are so dear to me—you have no idea! Well, when I first did them, I was (1) questioning the sanity of my English teacher and (2) scared to write anything incriminating. Some of my best work has come out of those things this year. They amplify how many things a person can have going on in their head at the same time. And I quote Sean Connery in *Finding Forrester* in saying: "The first step to writing is to write." The freewrites changed the way I wrote.

Emily's words are echoed again and again as I look through final reflections from my high school students in the years after I began using free writing regularly with them. They found the writings to be extremely powerful tools in their writing toolboxes. Though my original study began with older students, the findings definitely held true for high school.

A Lesson in Free Writing

On the second day of school, I spend the first 10 minutes of class reading to my students from the quotes you saw earlier in this chapter as well as from the third chapter of Anne Lamott's *Bird by Bird* (1994). I do my best to get them all jazzed up about free writing. I tell them Mike's story and get many nods as students recognize themselves in him. Then I make the following challenge:

> For the next 30 minutes, you may do nothing but write. You may write about anything that pops into your mind: in fact, I encourage you to record your thoughts as they are. Follow your thoughts wherever they take you. If you find yourself suddenly thinking about another topic, go with it. If you can't think of anything to say, write, "I can't think of anything to say." Whatever you do, do not stop writing for the entire 30 minutes.

After a moment or two for students to get comfortable, I start the timer and we all write. I am merciless in these 30 minutes. I write with the students while keeping an eye out for anyone who looks like they might stop for a break. Taking a break is not acceptable, and that quickly becomes clear.

At the end of the 30 minutes, as students stretch their fingers, dash to write down a few more words, and sigh with relief, I ask students to read through what they've written and underline or highlight anything that they like or just find surprising. I give them about 5 minutes to do so. I am always amazed at how relaxed and still the room is at that time. Besides being a great tool for invention, free writing is an amazing tool for calming and focusing students.

I then ask students to share their surprises and gems with a partner. Students are almost always eager to read, and the room fills with low murmurs punctuated by bursts of laughter. At the end of this session I introduce the first writing assignment of the year: an essay on anything of their choice. Most students are holding the topic in their hands by this time and are thoroughly sold on free writing. Others admit that they didn't take the exercise as seriously as they should have, but after hearing what happened for their classmates promise to go home and set the kitchen timer.

I must admit, the day I introduce students to the magic of free writing is on my short list of favorite classes. I see the fruits of that day over and over again throughout the year. *Powerful!*

The Last Word on Free Writing

The key is *comfort*. Students need to know that we are there to help them write something they are proud of rather than waiting in the wings with our red pens to point out their failures. The more they experience free writing without being penalized for making mistakes or wasting time, the more comfortable they will become. As they become comfortable, they will find those creative thoughts that the expository writing student shared with his professor. They will be able to follow Donald Murray's advice from *Write to Learn* (1999) for those trying to write: "Write now. Don't wait for an idea. . . . Don't worry about being silly or stupid or clumsy or accurate or sensible, not now. Outrun all the censors in your head" (p. 1).

DAYBOOKS: A PLACE TO STORE FREE WRITING AND THINKING

Though it may appear under many different names, the daybook is an essential tool for writers. *Daybook* is my favorite term for a notebook that contains the writer's thoughts and musings. Another widely used term is the *writer's notebook*. In fact, I think "writer's notebook" is a wonderful term to use for small children. The phrase can make them feel that they are truly a proud part of the writing community. I hesitate to use it with some older children for fear that they will be intimidated. Our teen-aged students tend to be much more skeptical; simply calling their notebook a "writer's notebook" is not enough to convince them that they are truly writers, and it may frighten them away. In my experience, struggling students at all levels are often very skeptical and have to be eased into the idea of thinking of themselves as writers. My best advice is to know your students and choose the term you wish to use based on that information.

I would, however, strongly caution teachers about using the terms *diary* or *journal*. There is too much pressure behind those words. I have heard countless people, students and adults, professional and nonprofessional writers echo my own feelings about the impossibility of keeping a journal or diary. *Diary* has the connotation of recording one's daily life. The problem here, as Dr. Sam Watson has pointed out in his classes, is the "sheer tedium with which many students seem to see their lives." His favorite example is "I had cornflakes for breakfast yet again this morning." Writing in a diary seems terribly boring.

If I am writing in a journal, I feel that each word should be perfectly formed and addressed to my children or grandchildren. These words must be immortal; they are an impression left of me! When I read back over what I have written, I find that it is boring, terrible drivel. Or it is shallow and silly, or it just plain doesn't make sense. I *hate* journals.

But I *love* my daybooks. The title of Ralph Fletcher's (1996) book on the notebook as a writer's tool sums it up nicely. He explains the title *Breathing In, Breathing Out* in the following manner:

> *Breathing In* refers to the way the notebook serves as a container for selected insights, lines, images, ideas, dreams, and fragments of talk gathered from the world around you. . . . *Breathing Out* suggests that the notebook is a fine place from which to take what you have collected and use it to spark your own original writing. (p. 2)

Fletcher's book and Donald Murray's *Write to Learn* (1999) are excellent resources for finding out more about how writers use their notebooks in their profession.

I was first introduced to the concept in the 1999 UNC-Charlotte division of the National Writing Project, and I doubt I will ever give it up. A co-leader of the writing project, Karen Haag, described it as a desk drawer—the place where you keep all of those little ideas that you have scratched on bits of paper, so that you may come back to work on them later. Karen and Nodghia Fesperman placed a 200-page Mead composition book and a glue stick in my hands and gave me permission to cut things apart and glue them to the pages.

At first the concept of cutting and pasting, jotting down notes on ideas, and writing bits and pieces as they came to me seemed a bit messy. When I learned to number each page and keep a running table of contents in the back, the mess turned into perfect order. The pages of the book could be as jumbled and disconnected as necessary. I could jump from idea to idea as often as the mood struck me. I could glue bits of napkin with an idea on it in the center of the page and write more notes all around it. I could write notes to myself about what I was thinking. I could explore a topic I wanted to write about. I could jot down a poem that was forming in my mind, or I could vent my frustrations and celebrate my successes. Looking through my daybooks, I see that some of what I have written is still silly, or selfish, or stupid, and yet ideal. Much of what goes in there will never be used, but the gems that do pop up are easily mined. What *power!*

The opening chapter for this book began in my daybook one day after I went running.

As I reached the end of my free write, I suddenly saw a connection between my running and my writing that had never occurred to me before. The whole framework for my book was born of these few pages. Many of the words from that free write actually appear in the book itself. I doubt I would have ever thought of the concept if I had not been in the habit of rambling about what was on my mind in my daybook (see Figure 1).

I also use my daybook to think about how to put ideas together. Chapter 3 of this book originally came from a section of an inquiry paper that I wrote at the beginning of my graduate school career. My professor applauded the ideas represented there, and I felt that they were important to what I was trying to say in this book. My first attempt at writing Chapter 3 was a disaster. I simply pasted bits and pieces from that paper together with some other aimless rambling. It was *awful.* I decided to paste the important concepts in my daybook and work with them there. I started to list what I wanted to say along with the pasted ideas, and mark up what I'd already written. Suddenly my brain was off and running. As you can see, I was calling it Chapter 4 at the time (see Figure 2).

I was able to begin rewriting the chapter after this exercise. When I came back to it later, I found an idea that I liked in my story about coaching, and I worked with it some more until it also appeared in the chapter. It didn't matter that the story was not all connected, or that it had to be carried over to another day. I can easily locate all of the story's bits and pieces by looking at the numbered pages, my own notes, and the table of contents.

Figure 1

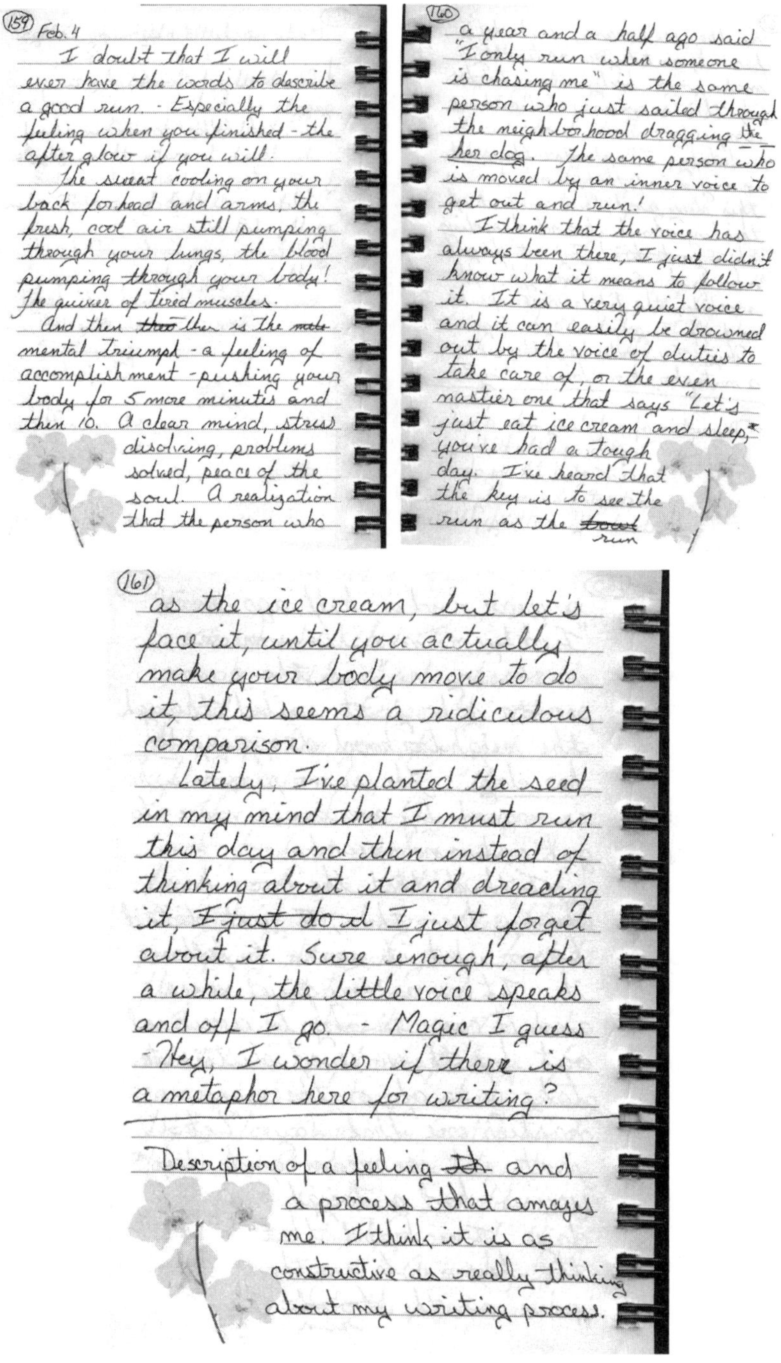

(159) Feb. 4

I doubt that I will ever have the words to describe a good run. Especially the feeling when you finished - the after glow if you will.

The sweat cooling on your back forehead and arms, the fresh, cool air still pumping through your lungs, the blood pumping through your body! The quiver of tired muscles.

And then ~~there is the~~ there is the mental triumph - a feeling of accomplishment - pushing your body for 5 more minutes and then 10. A clear mind, stress dissolving, problems solved, peace of the soul. A realization that the person who

(160) a year and a half ago said "I only run when someone is chasing me" is the same person who just sailed through the neighborhood dragging the her dog. the same person who is moved by an inner voice to get out and run!

I think that the voice has always been there, I just didn't know what it means to follow it. It is a very quiet voice and it can easily be drowned out by the voice of duties to take care of, or the even nastier one that says "Let's just eat ice cream and sleep, you've had a tough day. I've heard that the key is to see the run as the ~~boot~~ run

(161) as the ice cream, but let's face it, until you actually make your body move to do it, this seems a ridiculous comparison.

Lately, I've planted the seed in my mind that I must run this day and then instead of thinking about it and dreading it, ~~I just do it~~ I just forget about it. Sure enough, after a while, the little voice speaks and off I go. - Magic I guess - Hey, I wonder if there is a metaphor here for writing?

Description of a feeling ~~th~~ and a process that amazes me. I think it is as constructive as really thinking about my writing process.

Figure 2

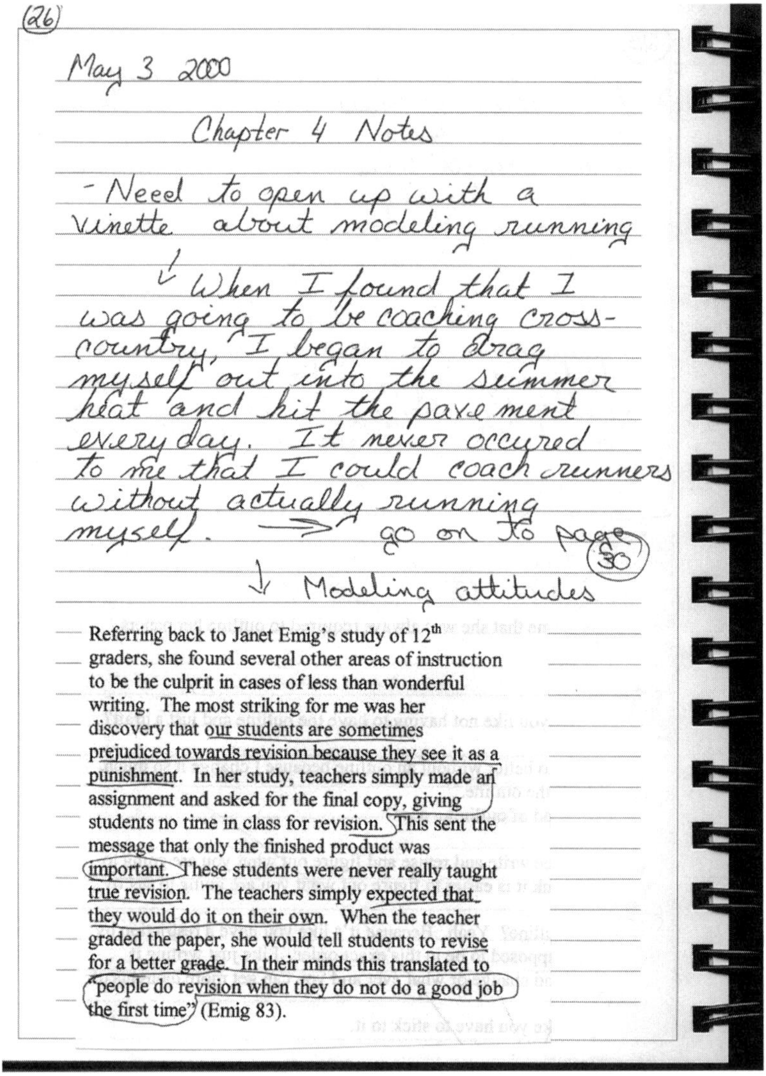

(26)

May 3 2000

Chapter 4 Notes

- Need to open up with a
vinette about modeling running

↳ When I found that I
was going to be coaching cross-
country, I began to drag
myself out into the summer
heat and hit the pavement
every day. It never occured
to me that I could coach runners
without actually running
myself. ⟶ go on to page ㉚

↓ Modeling attitudes

Referring back to Janet Emig's study of 12th
graders, she found several other areas of instruction
to be the culprit in cases of less than wonderful
writing. The most striking for me was her
discovery that our students are sometimes
prejudiced towards revision because they see it as a
punishment. In her study, teachers simply made an
assignment and asked for the final copy, giving
students no time in class for revision. This sent the
message that only the finished product was
important. These students were never really taught
true revision. The teachers simply expected that
they would do it on their own. When the teacher
graded the paper, she would tell students to revise
for a better grade. In their minds this translated to
"people do revision when they do not do a good job
the first time" (Emig 83).

As I modeled the use of my own daybook, my high school students came to use theirs for the same type of exploration. The free writing that they had learned to do in their daybooks began to carry over into other subjects and areas of their lives. In Figure 3, Elizabeth uses her daybook to explore a topic in history.

Figure 3

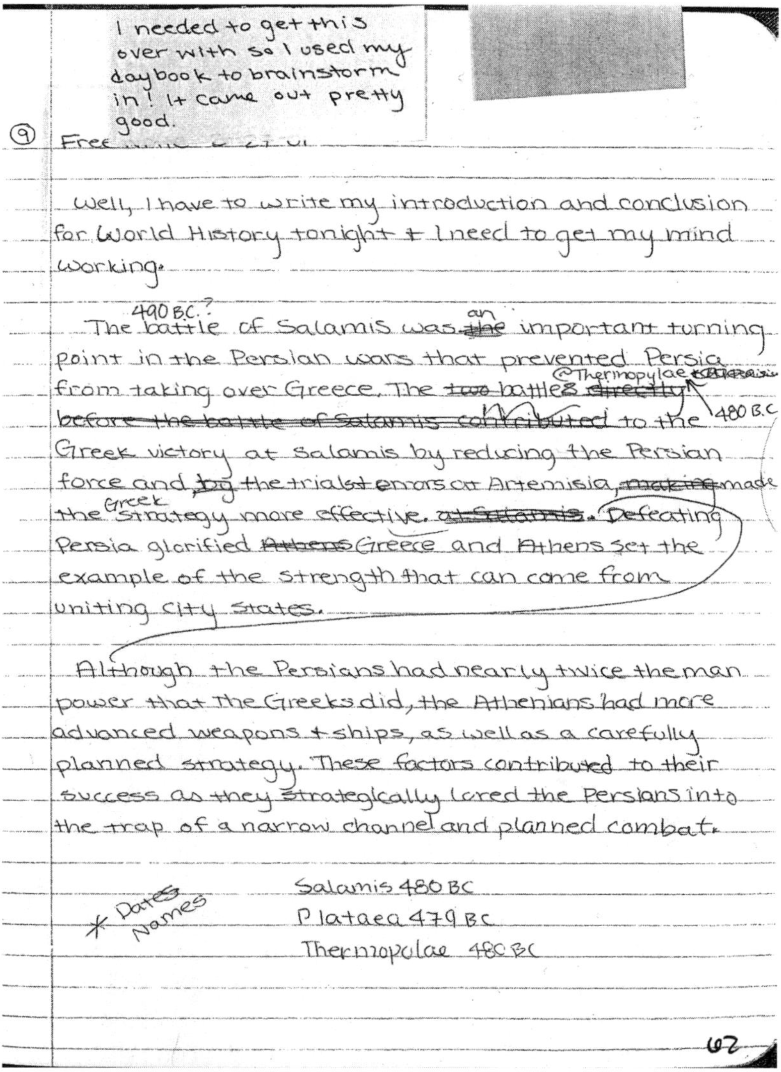

> I needed to get this over with so I used my daybook to brainstorm in! It came out pretty good.
>
> ⑨ Free write ~ 21 91
>
> Well, I have to write my introduction and conclusion for World History tonight + I need to get my mind working.
>
> 490 BC. ?
> The battle of Salamis was an important turning point in the Persian wars that prevented Persia from taking over Greece. The ~~two~~ battles ~~directly~~ @Thermopylae ~~& Artemisia~~ ~~before the battle of Salamis contributed~~ to the 480 B.C Greek victory at Salamis by reducing the Persian force and ~~by~~ the trials+ errors at Artemisia, ~~making~~ made the strategy more effective. ~~at Salamis~~. Defeating Persia glorified ~~Athens~~ Greece and Athens set the example of the strength that can come from uniting city states.
>
> Although the Persians had nearly twice the man power that the Greeks did, the Athenians had more advanced weapons + ships, as well as a carefully planned strategy. These factors contributed to their success as they strategically lured the Persians into the trap of a narrow channel and planned combat.
>
> * Dates Names
> Salamis 480 BC
> Plataea 479 BC
> Thermopylae 480 BC
>
> 62

Her daybook has become more than simply something she keeps for a grade in English class. It has become a writing tool for other areas as well. Looking at this bit of writing, we can see how Elizabeth "gets her mind working." By the end of the page, she knows what she will write her world history research paper about.

Many of my students even started to add things that didn't pertain to any class, just ideas, thoughts, things they were sorting through, all fodder for the creative pieces they would write later. When describing her writing process in a letter attached to a creative piece, Heather's words are quite typical of her classmates':

> Well, I started writing this on my computer, so there's little direct writing on my piece. Indirectly, there's a ton of free writes in my daybook about (ahem) the boys I mention in my paper, which shall remain nameless for the time being. If you really need to see them, let me know, but otherwise, trust me; I wrote WAY too much about them. (The first guy, at least, was a waste of space.)

Much of her thinking and prewriting happened in different places in her daybook. I love the way she says she "started the paper on her computer." Even though she had been doing all of this writing, it did not occur to her that it was a paper until the day she sat down at the computer. It is worth noting that "The Softest Lips in Kansas" is not the usual "teen-aged girl angst about boys" sort of story. It seems that Heather got all of that out of her system in her daybook and then went on to write a touching, sophisticated piece about self-actualization.

CONCLUSIONS

The daybook is much more than a place to do daily free writings that build fluency and voice. Free writing is more than simply writing about "whatever" for a period of time to rev up one's voice. Daybooks and free writing provide time and space to think and to explore those thoughts. If they are used correctly, they are wonderful writing tools. For free writing and the daybook to be valuable to students, students must use the writing they do there as a stepping stone to bigger pieces. These tools help writers warm up, but they are not the entire practice, and they certainly are not the race. If these writings are never referred back to or are never carried through the entire writing process, they are a waste of time, and students will see them as busy work. Keep reading to see where to go from here.

CHAPTER FIVE

The Practice Field

*Building Strength and Confidence
in Writing and Literary Analysis*

Anna is a high school junior. She runs cross-country and has a part-time job as a cashier at Eckerd's so that she can pay her parents back for her 1975 Volkswagen Beetle, put gas in it, and pay for the repairs that seem to be necessary every few months. Anna is taking honors courses and is very conscientious about her schoolwork. Her favorite subject is science, and she hopes to go to UNC–Chapel Hill on the premed track with a running scholarship. Anna is a very busy girl and is typical of many of our overachieving students.

Anna is distressed about her English class. It is her weakest subject, and her teacher, though a very nice woman, has decided that they should keep a journal in which to "flex and build their writing voices." The teacher is always going on and on about the necessities of building a writing habit and how, if they hope to become writers, they must practice every day. Anna doesn't want to become a writer; she just wants to do well enough in English to get into the AP course next year, pass the AP test, and be finished with writing for the rest of her life.

So far she is doing alright on the major papers, but the journal is really giving her trouble. She is supposed to find 10 minutes each night to write about something in addition to the essays that are assigned, the reading she needs to do, and the projects, assignments, and general homework from her other classes. What a pain! Luckily, her teacher only takes the journal up once a semester, and she gives a 1-week warning before that, so Anna knows she can catch up if she gets behind.

But Anna hates to get behind! She likes to know that all of her work is done before she goes to bed each night, and for the first 3 weeks, she managed to stay caught up with her journal entries. But then, there was that week where there was a big paper due in English, a test in chemistry, and a project in precalculus. After she made it home from cross-country practice, ate, and worked on her other homework, she was too tired even to think about writing. She was sure that she would be able to catch up on the weekend, but she had to work all day Saturday and Sunday, and by the time she ran on her own like Coach said (he would be able to tell if she didn't) and finished her homework for Monday, she just didn't get the journal entries done.

The following week, Anna did find time to make a few entries, but she never was able to catch up. As a matter of fact, she got more and more behind. It was just easier to put off the journal than the homework that was going to be collected and graded the next day. The week before the journals were due, Anna worked furiously in every spare second she had. When the day came, she turned in a completed journal.

The assignment was completed, an A was awarded, and everything turned out fine. Except, after a whole semester, Anna was no closer to developing the habit of writing or building fluency than she was the first day of class. To her, the journal was simply busy work given to her by a nutty teacher. She saw no use for it.

Most likely we would all consider Anna to be a good student. She prioritizes her busy life and has become quite adept at getting work done. But is she learning or just jumping through the hoops? She got very little out of all that writing except maybe a hand cramp and sleep deprivation. There was absolutely no connection in her mind between what she was writing and any of the other writing or reading she was doing in class.

Anna is certainly motivated by grades, so she probably would have written daily if she knew that her writing would be taken up and evaluated each day, but what teacher has time to do that? Besides, that would have defeated the purpose outlined by the teacher of "flexing the writing muscles." Anna is so grade conscious it is likely she would have taken very little risk in this writing.

But what if there had been time in class each day for journal writing? What if there were 10 or 15 minutes of the class period where the students actually did flex those writing muscles? And what if students understood that they could use their writing to think about what they read or about a paper that they were going to write? I would be willing to bet that with no distractions and no alternative assignments that she could be doing at that time, plus a purpose for writing, Anna would have written. And as she wrote each day, she would come to see at least a little bit of the value in the writing habit.

After all, her coach did not grade her each day on what she did on the practice field. He was just there to be sure that she was running and pushing herself to the best of her ability. His evaluation could come from watching her, but also from seeing the growth and progress she was making. That's how he could tell if she had taken 2 days off over the weekend. Anna would practice on her own for him, because she understood the value of it.

Our students need time to practice in class because there we can create a distraction-free environment. Though they may not understand their own need for sustained writing time or examination of their own reactions to the literature they read at first, as they build muscle and stamina, they will come to understand the value of both.

TYPES OF PRACTICE

There are many ways to build muscle while writing. The free writing that I discussed in the previous chapter is my personal favorite. They can free write on focused topics. They can write about their lives, what they are doing today, to find a focus line for an essay or a story, or to understand a piece of literature they are reading. Whether or not students are being allowed to practice their writing can also be determined by whether or not they are allowed to draft assignments in class that will eventually be graded, or by the order and nature of assignments. Practice in writing does not stop with the starting point, the searching that happens when a person is trying to look for a topic. A classroom that allows time for students to practice their craft is one that emphasizes process over product—the *entire* process. Simply assigning daily practice writing, taking it up, and grading it isn't enough. Students need to use that writing like real writers do. It needs to grow into something bigger; otherwise the students will see it as busy work, and rightly so. A classroom that works as a practice field is permeated with the following concepts:

1. Invention

2. Revision and drafting

3. Varied assignments in progression

Reader Response and Invention

Some of you are thinking, "Okay, my students have this daybook and they are exploring their thoughts through free writing. Very nice, but what about all of the literature I have to teach?" The daybook is also an excellent tool in the literature classroom. Students can learn about literature by writing about it in a non-threatening way in their daybooks using a technique commonly called "reader response." The more I read about free writing, the more I thought about how it could help a student to make sense of what she reads. I had found in the past that students often either become overloaded by what they read, or they don't take the time to think about it. Free writing through reader response could give them a chance to sort through all of the material their brains are taking in or remembering as they read, and help them to decide what is most important.

Most of us have been there. We have assigned our favorite novel, and we are pretty sure that the students have read at least some of it. We saw them with the books, frantically reading in the hall before class started, and they know the wrath with which we will seize upon them if they do not. We try to open up the discussion and nothing happens. Twenty-five students stare at their desks, praying to various gods that we will not call on them. "How can this be?" we wonder to ourselves. "The story is directly related to their lives; how can they not want to talk about it?" We probe, we encourage, we ask thought-provoking questions, and finally one or two people, always the same ones, say something that everyone else decides to agree with only after seeing our reactions to it.

We throw up our hands in disgust and give a killer pop-quiz on the picky details of the novel. That will teach them to show up to class without having read! But now, we'll have to grade quizzes tonight instead of watching *ER*. Why do students have to make everything so difficult?

Reader response is a great way to get students to think on their own and to get the conversation flowing. And, yes, students will have a hard time if they haven't read. The trick is to get the kids to respond in writing so that they know they have something to say. The first response should take place before any discussion, so that students have nothing to rely on but themselves. In the beginning, the response can be any type of reaction; it does not have to be literary genius (Probst, 1988, p. 11). Milner and Milner (1999) see the initial response as "individual readers face-to-face with the text." As teachers, we should be looking for "unmediated, felt response to the text" (p. 83). Students should not worry about correctness here, because each person's response is colored by his or her own experience. Writing such a response gives students time to think through their reactions (remember the discussion of how free writing helps people think) without being influenced by others. They will also feel like they have something to share when the time for discussion does arise.

Take a look at the response in Figure 1 from a tenth grader's daybook after he has finished reading Book I of *Siddhartha* (Hesse, 1951/1998).

Eric often quotes songs or movies and draws in his initial thinking stages. These quotes and drawings get his brain working on what he is reading and give him a jumping-off point for discussion. His thoughts really got the ball rolling for our class. We had a rich discussion that day about the irony they saw in Eric's response juxtaposed with several other students' ideas about Siddhartha's inability to truly love. So much more exciting than grading pop quizzes!

We as teachers must be careful at this point to give equal attention to all responses in the discussion that follows the students' writing rather than only the ones that apply to our

Figure 1

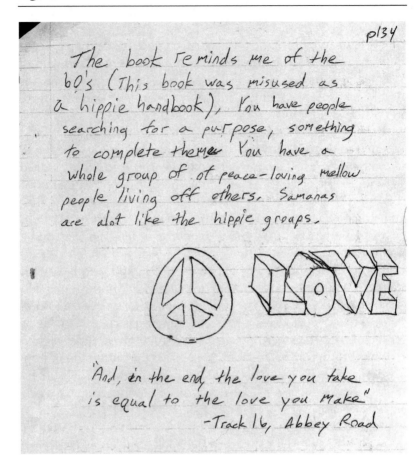

interpretation of the work. Even if I had not thought of hippies as I read *Siddhartha,* I needed to let that idea play out. Students will sense quickly whether or not their teacher is truly interested in their thoughts or is simply trying to support her own. As the discussion moves along, the students will more than likely be able to weed out problematic thoughts. After discussing these initial responses, we can move the students into deeper analysis by asking them to examine what exactly it was about the text that triggered those responses (Probst, 1988, p. 17).

The idea behind reader response is that first we need to get students to respond to a text on a personal level, much as Eric has. Then we can begin to talk about how the writing evokes such feelings and ideas, and then what the author *intended* for us to feel. Through these writings and conversations, we eventually come to the discussion of literary terms and conventions. Remember the "tone" lesson that emerged from the *Things Fall Apart* (Achebe, 1959) discussion in Chapter 3? When we jump straight into literary analysis, we are like baseball statisticians.

> When we substitute historical or critical questions for the direct experience of reading and reflecting, we are on the periphery. We are like baseball statisticians discussing batting averages—the discussion has to do with the game, but it is not the same as playing the game. No doubt some people will prefer the statistics to the game, but it is nonetheless important to perceive the distinction between the two and avoid confusing them in our teaching. The ball player and the statistician require different sorts of training. So do the reader and the literary scholar. (Probst, 1988, p. 8)

Few of our students are ever going to become literary scholars. Therefore, they see little purpose in studying literary conventions just for the sake of doing so. Students become engaged in literature through coming to care about what they are reading. According to Milner and Milner (1999), "When students are so engaged, questions of literary knowledge, such as conventions and literary terminology, can arise naturally out of student's push to understand texts more fully" (p. 85). The conventions that we all struggle to teach will come to be a natural curiosity to our students as they attempt to explore the text.

The following is an outline of the way that Probst (1999) suggests we move through the different levels of response.

1. Response
   Help students connect to the literature in their own way using individual thought cultivated but not provided by teachers:
   - Immediate, short written response
   - Small group or partner work
   - Large group discussion fostering multiple points of view

2. Working with the text directly
Help students decide what part or parts of the text caused them to have that response:
   - Short written response
   - Small group or partner work
   - Large group discussion to get many points of view

3. Thinking about author and purpose
Help students decide what the author was attempting to do with this piece and how he or she went about that. (Literary terms can be introduced and addressed here):
   - Short written response
   - Small group or partner work
   - Large group discussion to get many points of view (Probst, 1988)

These steps are certainly not a formula to be followed every single time we want to have a class discussion. Some days, students may need the security of small groups to get discussions started. Other days, students may come in overflowing with personal responses and be ready to discuss as a whole group immediately. Forcing the same steps every day would make for a deadly boring classroom. They are simply a framework to help us think of the types of informal writing we can have our students do in order to help them understand the literature they read and begin to talk about it.

A friend and colleague of mine, Lucy Perkins, began giving her students "5 minutes to be brilliant" before large group discussions. They would huddle in groups of three or four and sort out their responses and ideas. Discussions would begin with reports from each of these groups. After she began a class with these short group sessions, a few times the students began to come in and request "5 minutes to be brilliant" after a particularly challenging reading assignment. On those days, they needed to form ideas with a few people before moving out to the big group. As we give our students different avenues for practice in their thinking about literature, we are adding to their toolboxes, and eventually they will be able to pick and choose what they need to use depending on the reading and what they want or need to get out of it.

Another practical application of reader response is the following list of focused response topics. These are not the only topics that can be used; they are examples of the many different types of thinking that we can tap into using reader response. The list began as a handout given to me by Karen Haag during the writing project. I adapted it to fit my classroom and then added other items suggested by other teachers as well as by my own students.

A very important point is that *we as teachers must have a firm concept of the theory behind our practice.* Simply throwing one of these response ideas in as a time filler is a waste. We must know where we are headed at all times. We must ask, "How am I helping my students stretch and build their writing, reading, and thinking muscles today? How is this activity contributing to the overall goal, and how is it connected to what we did yesterday? Last week?" Otherwise, we are no better than Anna's well-intentioned but misguided teacher.

In terms of the following focused response list, I want you to see the purpose behind each topic. Remember the proficient reader strategies from Chapter 3? Many of the topics give students practice in those areas. Some of the topics take students on to the next level, which Milner and Milner (1999) call "formal analysis" (p. 106). Formal analysis is the level at which students start to really think about the way a text is put together. Those focused response topics are a superior alternative to lecturing about literary terms and conventions.

Focused Reader Response

1. Write a conversation between you and another student about the reading. (Synthesizing)

2. Think about someone you know. Write a letter from their perspective about what it would be like to know you if you began to behave like a character of your choice from this story. (Inferring)

3. Write a letter to the author about what you have read. (Asking Questions of Authors)

(Continued)

(Continued)

4. Quote parts of your reading and explain why you liked the quotes you chose. *Or,* be specific about what you didn't like in the reading. (Determining Important Ideas)

5. Make a list of the main points of the chapter. Write a letter to a friend explaining the importance of these points. (Determining Important Ideas)

6. Rewrite the reading as a poem. (Synthesizing)

7. Draw the movies of your mind as you read. (Creating Sensory Images)

8. Write about a memory the reading jogged in your mind. (Activating Prior Knowledge—Text to Self)

9. Rewrite the story or event as a Monty Python script. (Synthesizing)

10. Compare the reading you have done with another similar reading. (Activating Prior Knowledge—Text to Text)

11. Compare the ideas you have learned from the reading that you have done to the ideas expressed by a person who would disagree. (Activating Prior Knowledge—Text to World)

12. Write using an idea of your own that will help you deepen your understanding of the reading. (Activating Prior Knowledge—Text to Self)

13. Chart the ideas or events you have found in your reading. (Determining Important Ideas)

14. Write your own poem mimicking the style of the author. (Formal Analysis)

15. Transport a character from your reading to the present and describe five prize possessions they would own based on what you know about their personality. (Inference)

16. Write about how the writer began this chapter. How did she get you interested? What particular phrases or events pulled you into the book? What made you keep reading? (Formal Analysis)

17. What makes the character likable, believable, or strong willed? What details are used to describe the character? What makes you admire him or her? (Formal Analysis)

18. Take a look at how the author develops a character. Look at four areas:
    - What does the character do in this story that reveals his or her personality? Record the actions of the character.
    - What does the character say? Record actual words spoken by the character.
    - What does the author say about the character? Record the actual phrases or words from the text.
    - What do other characters say about the main character? Record actual phrases. (Formal Analysis)

19. What do you think the theme of the story is? Record actual quotes or events that will help you prove your theory. (Synthesizing)

20. Write a letter to the author about the questions your reading leaves you with. (Questioning the Author)

The most important thing about all of these topics is that they engage the students with the literature, and they get them writing about it. All of them also give students practice with important reading strategies. But again, simply assigning one of these is not enough. The assignment must eventually work into something bigger. The "something" can be as simple as discussion or as complex as a published writing.

Writing Project Co-Leader Nodghia Fesperman did a presentation on reader response in which she showed us how she sometimes moved her senior English classes through the different levels of response:

Reader Response

> *Please write in paragraph form.*

Summary
- Get the gist.
- Read literally.
- Avoid ambiguities.
- Avoid personal opinions.
- Use third person pronoun.

Response
- Give personal reactions to text.
- Consider the language of the text.
- Ponder what the text means.
- Use first person pronoun.

Connection
- Relate the text to your personal experience, to literature, to history, to movies, and/or to television.

Fesperman's exercise immediately takes the reader from plot summary to response to connection in the space of a 15-minute writing assignment. The directions she gives concerning point of view give students clues about their relationship to the text as readers. First they are just retelling the story, then reacting to it, and then connecting it to their own experiences. It accomplishes the same goals as Probst's (1988) line-up in a much more succinct fashion. These writings could easily lend themselves to both large and small group discussion as well as to larger pieces of writing.

Another form of reader response that was introduced to me in the writing project was based on Ann Berthoff's double-entry journal.

Double-Entry Response

1. Fold page in half "hot dog style."
2. Reserve left side for "note taking."

      a. Quote
      b. Summary
      c. Statistic
      d. Definition

3. Reserve right side for response.
      a. Significance of quote
      b. This reminds me of . . .
      c. This is important because . . .
      d. I'll use this when . . .

Double-entry responses allow students to have the text on one side of the page and their response to it on the other. It forces them to make decisions about what parts of the text are important enough to write down. Then it requires them to immediately justify that point by writing about it in the other column. Students must learn what parts of text are significant in order to become proficient readers. It is a very time-consuming task, but it allows students to practice skills that they will need to write literary analysis and actually begin that analysis. It is particularly useful for difficult text that requires the reader to break it down into small chunks in order to understand it.

My students particularly like double-entry responses for gathering quotes and ideas when they know that they will eventually be writing formal essays about a piece of literature. They often find topics in their musings, and then the quotes that prompted those thoughts are right there in their daybooks for support.

We can add one other dimension to the double-entry journal with the dialectic response.

Dialectic Response Journal

1. Create four columns in your notebook.

2. Reserve Column 1 for "note taking."
      a. Quote
      b. Summary
      c. Question about the text

(Continued)

(Continued)

3. Reserve Column 2 for your response to Column 1.
   a. Think about the significance.
   b. Think about the author's purpose.
   c. What is causing you to have this question about the text?

4. Reserve Column 3 for a response from another person.
   a. Agree/Disagree
   b. Extend
   c. Question

5. Reserve Column 4 for "What I'm Thinking Now."
   a. Ideas solidified
   b. New questions raised
   c. Questions answered
   d. New ideas

I have found that having that third column for peer commentary works wonders with students who are having trouble truly discussing literature among themselves. Responding in writing to each other's thoughts gives the students a starting point for discussion. Later when they return to their dialectic responses to mine ideas for writing, they see the value of recording such discussions.

Using different forms of reader response, we can generate a much more lively and authentic discussion about literature with our students while at the same time giving them that practice writing time that they so desperately need. Because they have time to write and think about the literature before they have to speak, their ideas will be more solidly formed, and they will feel that they really have something to say. All the while, the students are developing fluency in their writing.

And there is one more added benefit as well. Think of all of the types of reader response that you have seen so far and all of the topics that you have been coming up with on your own as you read these. Imagine what kinds of writing your students will do in their daybooks about the literature they read. Not only are they getting regular practice with writing, but they are also practicing writing about literature. Imagine students tackling an essay assignment. Their writings will be a wonderful resource for them.

They will have already done quite a bit of thinking and planning about the topic before it is even assigned. Better yet, allow them to pick their own topics. Their daybooks should be filled with ideas they can draw from. The beautiful literary writings from my tenth graders that I mentioned in Chapter 3 came in part from such collections in students' daybooks.

Remember that writing test that we give tenth grade English students in North Carolina? The test asks students to read two quotes and then write an editorial using those quotes and literature they have read on an issue given to them on the test. The students are given 100 minutes to accomplish the task. Many of my colleagues see the test as a road block to the kind of writing and thinking discussed here. But think of how well-prepared students who are continually engaged in forming their own responses and judgments about literature will be, compared to those who simply spit back a teacher's words in essay form. A student who knows how to think about literature will do well on such a test, as well as on reading comprehension tests.

Reader response accomplishes three major goals of the literature-based high school English class:

1. Done correctly, it increases reading comprehension by allowing students to practice proficient reader strategies.

2. It gives students a springboard for writing longer pieces about literature by allowing them to do a good bit of thinking beforehand.

3. It gives students time to practice and hone their writing skills in a nonthreatening environment.

Using reader response, students can take risks, explore, play with words, and strengthen their voices as they write about what they have read or the things that they are reminded of by that reading.

In-Class Drafting and Revision

Time in Class

One of the most obvious, but most often ignored, types of writing practice in the classroom is that of allowing and requiring students to go through the steps of the writing process *in class.*

When we do not allow time for drafting and revision in our classrooms, our students do not see them as important parts of writing. Instead they see anything short of pouring a perfect paper onto the page the first time as imperfect or as downright "bad" writing.

My students speak often about how much drafting and getting comments on those drafts helps them. Eventually they realize that by drafting and revising, they are able to see what is working for them, and they learn to apply the lessons from one piece of writing to the next.

All writers, including student writers, need to draft out and revise their work. Students also need nongraded feedback on these drafts. As one student so aptly put it, "You don't feel as pressured," and I am convinced that lack of pressure eventually equals better writing. As teachers, many of us may be hesitant to give up the pressure of a grade for fear that our students will not take the writing seriously. Again, I say that we must trust our students, but I also feel that such an issue is a great reason for allowing class time for at least some of these drafts, especially the initial ones. After the students get into what they are writing and have real reasons for wanting to develop it and make it better, they will put the time and effort into the writing on their own.

Allowing time for the initial drafting in class goes back to the same principle as allowing those informal daybook entries in class. If we give students time when they can do nothing but write, they will be more likely to do it. As my students have pointed out, revision is not something many students do on their own. By having students write with us, we can ensure an environment that will be without distraction or alternative to the actual writing.

Another benefit of allowing class time for drafting and revising is that we will be there to help and encourage students through the rough spots. As students work with and build new writing skills, they are certain to become frustrated at times. If they are experiencing frustration all alone, they are more likely to quit. They may or may not ask us about how to move forward the next day when they come to class. Allowing time to work in class ensures that we will be there to offer advice and encouragement as students need it. (I discuss more about what to do with in-class revision time in Chapter 7, on conferencing.)

Revision Strategies

In-class drafting also gives us a chance to help our students shake up their writing and truly resee it. I typically have 2–3 writing workshop days for each writing assignment that my students take all the way to publication. Somewhere in that cycle the writing they do in the first 10 minutes of class comes from the list following:

Revision Strategies/Ideas

1. Write two new introductions.

2. Write two new conclusions.

3. Switch the point of view (from first to third person or from third to first person).

4. Add dialogue where you have just description of an event.

5. Rewrite your conclusion as the introduction and then write a new conclusion.

6. Write a dialogue with a friend describing your paper, telling why you thought it was important, and what you thought was important.

7. Create a stream of consciousness about what is going on beneath the surface of the action or arguments or explanations.

8. Describe a place alluded to in the paper, using all five of your senses.

9. Create an opening that starts in the midst of the action.

10. Describe a person mentioned in the paper.

11. Describe what happens after the paper ends.

12. Describe what happened before the events of the paper.

13. Describe a personal experience related to an argument in the paper.

(Continued)

(Continued)

14. Argue from your opponent's point of view.

15. Create a dialogue representing two or more points of view.

16. Write an argument as a narrative.

17. Write an analysis as a letter to a friend.

18. Write a formal argument as a stream of consciousness.

19. Write to a different audience—Miss Piggy, for instance.

20. Write a formal argument as a poem in two voices.

21. Put your draft aside and write a quick outline of the points you want to make.

22. Color coding:
    a. Complete number 21 from the list.
    b. Color-code *each* point.
    c. Read your paper and color-code each sentence based on the point it best supports.
    d. Organize your paper by color.

Students who have been with me for a while have a copy of this list in their daybooks to reference when they know they need to revise and can't figure out how to get started. When I first introduce revision, I pick and choose several items from the list that I know will be helpful for the writing my students are doing. The goal is eventually to expose students to the entire list and teach them to choose what will work best for the piece of writing they are working with that day. It's great fun to see what students find through these writings, and the list coupled with class time for revision all but eliminates drafting that solely involves changing one or two words.

Types and Progression of Assignments as Practice

Another way to allow students practice time in writing is by closely monitoring the progression of assignments. We want to help our students build confidence as well as skills throughout the course of the year. Practicing the same type of writing assignment over and over again throughout the course of the year may help students learn that style of writing, but it does little to help them become better writers in all situations. Any confidence students gain in that one style will disappear when they are faced with something different.

Writing From Experience

I have found that it is easiest for students to write from their own experience. Think of those golden moments when you have snatched a few seconds of time away from the literature curriculum and allowed students to write about their own lives. Some of the richest writing I have ever received from students came from such assignments. The key is that the students have a choice about what they are writing, and they are writing on a topic that they are quite familiar with: themselves and their experiences. They can simply focus on using words and crafting their language to get their point across. Writing from one's own experience is extremely important to the developing as well as the developed writer.

Our students' experiences have a definite place in the literature classroom, as we have already seen in the reader response section. Events in the stories we read in class may trigger a memory for a student. Often these memories become topics for further writing. Certainly we would not want to limit our students' writing about literature to personal responses, but we cannot exclude them either.

Mimic and Imitation Writing

We can also use experience writing to check for student mastery of literary forms through imitation assignments. Instead of having students write test essays about the style of a particular author, have them mimic that style. To accomplish such a task will require a firm understanding of the conventions the author used and bring purpose to a discussion of those conventions (Dellinger, 1982, p. 41). The result will be richer writing and more thorough understanding of literary terms and concepts. In addition to making their writing much more interesting to read, giving students opportunity to write fiction, drama, or poetry allows them to "face the same choices authors face. They address questions of form as practical matters, not as theoretical ones" (Milner & Milner, 1999, p. 115). And suddenly, once again, literary terms and conventions become a useful thing for our students rather than simply something that Teacher wants them to memorize.

I have found imitation writing to be a particularly powerful tool in my classroom. One of my favorite assignments of the year was my final exam for my Basic English 10 class in 2001.

Final Exam
Basic English 10

All year we have been discussing what we can learn about a culture through the study of its literature. In *Night* we learned about the Jewish culture and the struggle of these people during the holocaust. Through *Oedipus* we learned of the great pride of the ancient Greeks as well as their system of government. As we waded through *Les Miserables,* we learned about life in France after the French Revolution. The list goes on. Add to that all of the literary terms and conventions we have learned about that the authors used to get their point across. You've really learned quite a bit this year!

The Exam

You will have two hours to describe what you consider to be your own culture and then write a short story or long poem that you feel shows your culture. You have the next week to think about and plan what you are going to write. On the day of your exam, you will turn in all brainstorming and planning that you have done as a part of your grade. Use what you have learned to create something you will be proud of!

Lamont was in English 10 for the second time. He transferred into my class in the middle of the first semester with less than stellar recommendations from his teacher. We got off to a rocky start, but slowly we came to respect one another. He found himself taking my final exam and needing a good grade. He was in danger of failing because of a lengthy suspension. His essay describing his culture begins:

> You can smell the salmon and rice all the way down the street, either that or Roger's little brother cryin' behind getting a whoopin' for playing with the oven door. It's only about ten o'clock the first Monday of summer break.

And for two pages he writes a beautiful creative essay switching between Black vernacular and standard English in all the appropriate areas. Not only has he described his culture, he has put us in the moment. He also demonstrates that he has learned how important the use of dialect can be to a descriptive piece of writing, while proving that he is proficient in standard English.

Now, take a look at his poem:

Just Enough

Life's a B and then you die

between all the bull a little happiness sometimes crying

Walk out the crib everyday the hood seems like it dying

stay in school don't be a fool was what I heard from older heads

how you go tell me something and you can't rent you head

Show all the respect in the world like changing to women from a girl

let 'em know the sheets ain't my world

Even tho' the chronic and deep ebonies make you reminisce

other days it's hot everybody got an attitude even the dogs are pissed

but I love this

I take as a challenge

Try not to get young like Frankie Voleny

Let my little brother know the streets don't last for eva'

One day sooner or later we'll all eat together

At a table at the same time no watching t.v.

With my little sister on her way to college little CiCi

That's 8 or 9 years down the line but keep dreamin' and quite schemin' and just try

My open window to the world is apartment with no screen door

I been through 'bout quitin' I was like "Why try fo'"

Forget all the projects and the bling bling

I'm a always stay real and strive for my dreams!

Wow! As I sat reading exams on that steamy, hectic afternoon in early June, I had no doubt that Lamont had learned about the importance of literature as a window into different cultures. He also knew how to express his thoughts in a powerful way in writing. Had I asked for a standard test essay on the same topic, I doubt the result would have packed the same punch. As a matter of fact, this student may not have even done it. My exam allowed him to show me what he had learned rather than trying to find out what he had not learned. By allowing him to *practice* all that he had learned for the year rather than *reciting* that knowledge, I gave him a chance to do something meaningful, and it paid off. While other teachers were grumbling standing in line at the Scantron machine lamenting over the fact that their students hadn't studied and that they were never going to get their grades done, I was curled up on the couch in the lounge reading wonderful literature written by my students. It was a positive experience for all of those involved.

Another type of assignment that was born out of the imitation assignment is what I like to call "the translation." It comes in handy when we are wading through difficult or ancient texts. The example here is from a unit about Greek tragedy and *Oedipus Rex*. The assignment was to pick a scene in *Oedipus* and rewrite it for the movies. The students were told that they could change anything they felt necessary to make the scene interesting to today's audiences without altering Sophocles' original story. The purpose here is not only to show understanding of the intricacies of *Oedipus Rex*, but also how drama has changed over thousands of years. Many students find Greek drama silly, with all of its "rules." The following piece shows Elisha's understanding that American drama has rules as well. The rule here: We love a good chase scene.

"Oedipus and Tiresias"
Adapted from Sophocles' "Oedipus Rex"

Oedipus is on stage. Tiresias arrives, feeling his way around blindly. He hobbles.

Oedipus: Ah, Tiresias, good to see you here.

Tiresias: But I don't want to be here.

Oedipus: But you need to be here! The people of Thebes are dying, seer. We need your insight to help us find the murderer of Laius.

Tiresias: You do not want to know the murderer of Laius! You are a fool to ask.

Oedipus becomes outraged and runs over to Tiresias and hits him. Tiresias falls to the ground; Oedipus quickly picks him up and pins him against the wall.

Oedipus: How dare you insult me in my own palace! *[tightens grip]*

Tiresias: *[gasping]* Is this—any—way to—treat a—blind—man?

Oedipus hesitates, then lets go.

Oedipus: Tell me now who killed the great Laius, or tell me that you are a false seer!

Tiresias: I am not a false seer, and I will not tell you!

Oedipus: You yourself are a fool to be so stubborn. Do you know what fate you face if you continue to seal your lips?

Tiresias: No, but I should like to hear.

Oedipus: The same as the murderer will himself endure—death or exile!

Tiresias: On what grounds?

Oedipus: I am King, I need no grounds; but treason will do.

Tiresias: Hah! You do not frighten me. In fact, I am glad that it's less of a fate than yours.

Oedipus: Old man, stop playing games, else you will cause the deaths of many more of my innocent subjects who are at this very moment suffering and dying.

Wailing and moaning sounds heard off in the distance.

Tiresias: *[pauses, looks both saddened and distressed]* I must go now
. . . *[begins walking away]*

Oedipus: No, blind fool, you cannot go! How dare you deprive
Thebes of the answers it deserves! Don't you understand
that your silence causes pain?

Stops, turns around slowly.

Tiresias: Oedipus, my friend; pain is the very reason why I hold my
breath.

Oedipus: Surely it cannot be more painful than what my people are
feeling now. Come, tell!

Tiresias: *[pauses, then lurches toward door and practically runs out]*

Oedipus: Guards! Bring me that man!

*Chase scene ensues. Tiresias runs down a curving staircase, stumbling
over many steps and finally tumbling at the base (the music is roaring by now,
of course). He runs down a hallway at full mark, swaying his staff out side to
side to avoid obstacles. He gets to a door and fumbles for the knob. He finds it
and yanks the door open and runs smack into the shelving (it's a closet). He
runs to the next door, which leads outside, and again runs down some steps
(but this time more carefully). The guards, meanwhile, are running about 30
feet behind him. He finds a road and begins to run, again swaying his staff to
check for obstacles. However, the staff gets stuck in the wheel of a passing char-
iot, and it provides a hard blow to his shins. He falls down in the dirt awk-
wardly and is taken away by the guards. Scene changes back to palace setting,
with guards dragging Tiresias inside. They drop him on the floor and he shouts
out in pain.*

Oedipus: You don't learn a lesson very well, do you?

Tiresias: *[gasping for air]* Neither do you.

Oedipus: Now will you tell me the name of the rogue that killed
Laius, or shall I wait until you break something else?
You know, I am beginning to suspect that your silence
hides something. Could it be that you had a part in the
murder?

Tiresias:	No, it is not true, and to prove it so I will promptly tell you the real perpetrator . . . even though you do not want to know.
Oedipus:	I want to know, so tell me!
Tiresias:	No, Oedipus, you do not want me to tell, for the culprit is you yourself!
Oedipus:	The culprit of what? Of searching for truth?
Tiresias:	No, of murder! You are the one who killed Laius, and—
Oedipus:	What, are you saying I killed the king of the land which I now rule? Such blasphemy!
Tiresias:	It's only the truth.
Oedipus:	It's only a lie! You know I did not do it, and you simply want me out of the crown for some purpose of yours. But what purpose would it serve you? Unless—
Tiresias:	Unless what?
Oedipus:	*[hits Tiresias again]* I knew you were a traitor! You have insulted me doubly, and now you tare to interrupt me? You really are a fool.
Tiresias:	I know not what you mean.
Oedipus:	Of course you do! Creon hired you to bring my unjust conviction, so that he may steal my position of power. What did he promise you, huh? His old job?
Tiresias:	There is nothing of the sort!
Oedipus:	I would have you tell the truth, but I think I've heard enough from you.
Tiresias:	I already told the truth, Oedipus, and I'm sure you'll find that out soon enough.
Oedipus:	Guards, show this blind man the door. The right door.

Tiresias is carried out. Oedipus remains, scene ends.

The dramatic irony of Sophocles' writing is preserved nicely in Elisha's writing, showing that he understands the literary element quite well. I must admit that watching these performances was much more interesting than reading a stack of dry essays on Greek dramatic conventions and dramatic irony.

Both of these assignments allow students to practice their newfound skills and use what they are learning about literature to create their own. The difference is the same as those between having a runner write an essay about the intricacies of running and having her actually hit the pavement and apply what she has learned.

Writing in a Series Toward Essay

"But don't students need to learn to write good essays at some point?" you may ask. Certainly! But remember we are talking about the practice field here, and all of these assignments are helping students build the writing muscles that they need for the essay, a much more difficult form for students to master. We have to move them there slowly. James Moffet (1981) has done quite a bit of study on different types of assignments and the best way to arrange them in order to help students grow and understand different genres of writing. He takes students through a series of assignments that begins with a form of reader response and moves finally into inference and, yes, the essay. He feels that by working through these steps with the same topic, students will be more successful in the higher-order thinking skills necessary for the essay. Take a look at his schema:

Recording what is happening	Drama	The chronologic of ongoing perceptual selection
Reporting what is happening	Narrative	The chronologic of memory selection
Generalizing what happens	Exposition	The analogic of class inclusion and exclusion
Inferring what will, may, or could be true	Logical Argumentation	The tautologic of transformation and combination

SOURCE: Moffet (1981, p. 13).

Following such a progression, students move through several different genres of writing while at the same time engaging in progressively deeper exploration of a topic. Topics for assignments can range from an observation of what happened in the school cafeteria, to a personal experience, to writing about a work of literature. No matter the topic, students are still moving from simply recording what they have seen, heard, or read to the much more sophisticated forms of writing and thinking required by forming one's own theory and then arguing to support it.

All too often we immediately ask students to generalize or infer from the literature they are reading when we ask them to write an essay. Often, they do not understand the work well enough to do this yet, or worse, simply have never been shown how to think about what they are reading on such an abstract level. Following Moffet's plan is one way to help them gain access to the literature and making generalizing and inferential writing more accessible to them. Dixie Dellinger (1982) wrote a book about designing writing assignments for high school based on Moffet's schema. She used his progression of assignments to get her students to write and think about a major theme in Shakespeare's *Othello.* My students and I enjoyed adapting the progression to our studies of *Night* (Wiesel, 1960).

NIGHT by Elie Wiesel

WRITING SERIES

Assignment One:

Write an interior monologue in which the character witnesses an act of inhumanity against another person. You may draw from personal experience or create a fictional persona and situation. (Reporting)

Assignment Two:

Write a dramatic monologue in which one person is telling another about what they saw in the first assignment. (Recording)

Assignment Three:

Write an article or essay that generalizes upon the subject of man's inhumanity to man—what it is and how it affects

(Continued)

(Continued)

> people. You may deal with general experience or you may write about the novel *Night*. (Generalizing)
>
> Assignment Four:
>
> Write an article or essay that develops a theory about man's inhumanity to man. You may use *Night* as a base or draw upon general experience. You may wish to consider such questions as:
>
> 1. The role of power in such situations
> 2. The role of culture and prejudices in such situations
> 3. Why such situations exist
> 4. Do we still see such inhumanity in our society? (Theorizing)

The last assignment smacks of the "theme paper" that is required by many standard courses of study, but think of how much more prepared the students will be to write it after going through the other assignments. Also, think of the wonderful surprises that will arise as the students work on their dramatic monologues in the first two assignments. How much more enticing these assignments look than the typical, "Explain how mans' inhumanity to man is a theme in *Night*." You may actually *want* to read these pieces! The progression can be easily adapted to just about any unit of study you are doing in your classroom.

Moffet's (1981/1982) theory and Dellinger's (1981) classroom adaptation of it provide an intriguing way for students to get into the literature they read and the events they are exposed to in life and write about them in progressively sophisticated forms. This progression allows students to build upon their own thoughts rather than simply jumping into critical thinking skills such as generalizing and theorizing. We take for granted that students already know how to think about what they have seen, heard, or read, or how that may change from another person's point of view in order to make generalizations. The truth is that many do not and are in dire need of practice in these areas. That practice makes the difference between those dry, seemingly identical essays and well-thought-out, original writing.

CONCLUSIONS

The practice field is the most important place in the development of athletes and writers. We must create such an atmosphere for our students by allowing them to practice and build muscle. Students learn by doing, so if they are to learn to write, we must allow them to do that as often as possible.

The mistake comes in thinking that a classroom that allows students to practice is not a rigorous one. We've all heard of those teachers who "don't make the kids do anything," and we certainly don't want to be labeled as one of *those.* I think of the students waiting outside my high school gym for rides after athletic practice. They are surprisingly quiet and still. They sit or lie on the metal benches looking as though picking up their hand would require more strength than they are capable of. When the ride comes, they slowly stand up, hoist the book bags onto their shoulders, stagger a little, and slowly make their way to the car. These students have only been practicing, but I guarantee they have worked hard! As long as we are requiring our students to think and develop as writers, they will be working hard as well.

I end here with a word of caution against using any of the suggestions and ideas in this chapter as isolated activities or time fillers. This is not to say that you must use each and every one of them, but to say that you must understand and be sure that the students understand the reasoning behind them. Daybook entries that are never used for larger writing assignments will soon become trivial to students and therefore a waste of precious time. Progressive assignments that build upon one another lose much of their value if students do not understand how they fit together. Graded writing assignments with no time for drafting or nongraded feedback will reinforce students' misconceptions about the writing process. Any of the assignments or ideas in this chapter used without an explanation of their purposes will be a waste.

It is up to us to explain the process of writing and reading to our students and then reinforce that explanation through our own actions, the assignments we make, and the ways we evaluate them. I say much more about standards and evaluation in the next chapter. For now, let us remember that teenagers are double-standard detectors. If we want them to take our classes seriously, trust us, and grow as writers and readers, then we must guard closely that they cannot detect any inconsistencies in what we say about writing and reading and what we do about each. If we are successful in getting them to trust us, we will be able to trust them. Once the trust is established, we will be able to work with and grow with our students as we all become better writers.

CHAPTER SIX

Race Day

Evaluation and the Idea of Grammar

On race days, I couldn't wait for school to end. I'd teach all day, tingling with the anticipation of the meet to come. When the gun fired, I watched each runner's start, hoping for the best, praying that all of the practice and advice from the week before would pay off. As the runners passed me, I shouted and encouraged each one, rooting them toward their personal goals. Some aspired to finish in the top three; others simply wanted to run the entire race. No matter the goal, they were all equally important.

When the race was over, we celebrated our victories and discussed our defeats. Then we put our heads together to figure out what needed to happen in practice in order to ensure better results for the next time. I came home on those nights feeling exhilarated, ready to take on the world and excited about the next day's practice.

I've learned to evaluate my students' writing in the same way. I look for the successes and talk with writers about ways we can create more. If you have been reading through *Using the Workshop Approach in the High School English Classroom* chapter by chapter, you may be wondering how I expect you to grade the amount of writing I am recommending you assign. Let me assure you that I do not! If we read and grade every single piece of writing that our students create, we will defeat the whole purpose of having them write daily. It will no longer be practice, but performance.

As English teachers, we often feel that it is our duty to carefully read all that our students write, painstakingly note each and every mistake they make, and then place a grade on the top of the page before handing it back. No wonder we have the reputation for being so cranky!

I agree with Tom Romano (1987) when he says that the purpose of a grade for writing should be to reflect the growth that student has undergone, make the student want to write again, and give students credit for the good-faith effort they have put into the piece (p. 128). A paper marked F, with red ink dripping from every page, is certainly not going to accomplish any of these goals. A grade on a paper that has been taken through the entire writing process should reflect how well the student used that process, how much growth has occurred, and also how effective the final product is. We also need to keep in mind that not every piece of writing should go all the way through the writing process. For example, if I were using Dellinger's (1982) series of assignments on a novel, I may have the students pick one to carry through to publication. The others may go into a portfolio of work on that novel. Or, they may simply go into the student's writing folder, to be returned to when the student is looking for ideas for their next published piece (just as the pros keep folders of ideas to work on later).

The way we evaluate writing is crucial, because it can negate all that we've been doing to help our students come to see themselves as real readers and real writers, or it can solidify that concept for them. We must take far more into account than correct grammar and usage when we grade student writing, but before we move into a discussion of those other items, I take a moment to explain where grammar fits in the workshop-based classroom. It is an integral part of all of our reading and writing.

GRAMMAR IN CONTEXT

The subject of evaluating student writing cannot be broached without bringing up the question of grammar instruction. If we aren't going to bleed papers red as we mark all of the mistakes, then what? They *have* to learn, don't they?

I have spent some time struggling with my own ideas about grammar. As a matter of fact, originally, I didn't have a chapter on grammar for this book. I didn't feel like I had much of a grammar background. I was in elementary school in the early '80s, which means that I had very little grammar instruction in school. I do remember doing some diagramming in seventh grade and hating English because I just couldn't get it. I took an entire course on diagramming in college. I made an A, but I couldn't diagram the sentence I've just written if my life depended on it. However, I can write grammatically correct sentences, free from coma splices, precariously dangling participles, and misplaced modifiers. Though my family has been known to use constructions like "I ain't got no . . ." and "Where is he at?" in conversation, I've never used them in formal writing, just as I do not use the phrase *chester drawers* to describe the object in which I put my clothes.

I do remember getting papers back with red ink dripping in school. If the mistakes affected my grade, I was more careful with my proofreading for the next paper. If it didn't, I disregarded the marks because they obviously weren't important. But what did I get marked down for? Who knows! For the life of me I can't remember. When I proofread the next paper, I simply made sure that it sounded right. So, how did I do it? Was I born with an innate knack for language? That would be a possibility, except for the fact that I can't retain foreign language to save my life and my spelling is atrocious. I wrote and proofread based on what sounded and looked right.

And that's the key! How did I know what sounded and looked correct? I'm a reader. I've been reading for as long as I can remember. Some of my earliest memories revolve around my mother, my brother, and me all piled in her rocking chair sharing a book. My mother read, my brother read, and I read even before I understood the words. I would hold the book, turn the pages, and make up the parts I couldn't remember. We made regular visits to the library and brought home as many books as we could carry. Before family vacations, we visited the library so that we would have plenty of reading to pass the time in the car. My brother and I even built a tree house in a cedar tree in the back yard so that we could read outside in the summer.

I knew how the written word should look and sound because of my experience with it. I didn't need to know what a modifier was in order to use one. When I wrote, I chose from the vast resources of words, phrases, and sentences that I had in my head.

Sure, there was some nudging along the way. Little lessons like the difference between *its* and *it's*, or *where* and *wear*, things that I needed to know in order to convey what I wanted to say, but that's why I learned them, because they did precisely that.

When I began teaching, I was at a loss about exactly how to teach grammar. I decided to focus on literature and writing, and as I'm sure you know from your own classrooms, that was enough to keep us busy. When papers came in, I marked them up for grammar and usage mistakes, graded them down—10 percent of the grade was grammar—and handed them back. The next paper would have the same mistakes, and I would mark them, sigh, and give them back. I *hated* grading papers for grammar, and my frustration about the grammar translated into hatred of grading the papers. There was no excitement on race day.

Ironically, in 1996—the first year of my teaching career—*English Journal* published an entire edition on grammar. Through all of the activities that I saw and read about, a theme emerged. Grammar instruction should be individualized and meet the kids where they are. I tucked these ideas away in my head and thought about using some of them. I know I intended to get those grammar books out that first year, but we simply ran out of time. The breakthrough came with the success of one student at the very end of the year. I can still see him, a young black man who sat in the first row in fifth period. He was a good kid with great ideas, but he had a major problem with sentence fragments. I began to work with him one on one. Together, we went through an entire paper, correcting the fragments and talking about what they were and why. The next paper looked as if a different person had written it. It was almost mistake free after only a half-hour spent outside of class. All of the grammar worksheets in the world couldn't have accomplished what we had in that afternoon. The key was that we were working with *his* words and *he* was ready to hear it.

The Bottom Line on Grammar

Many of your students don't have the benefit of an environment filled with books like I had growing up. And as high school English teachers, we don't have the luxury of extra time in our curriculum. It is ridiculous to waste valuable time that our students could be using to read and write by making them do grammar book exercises and diagram sentences. Instead, we must meet them where they are and provide them with the instruction they need as they need it. There is a plethora of research out there about the validity of such practices if the intent in teaching grammar is to improve writing. The most valuable to me has been Constance Weaver's *Teaching Grammar in Context* (1996). She takes her readers through all of the theory and research that has been done in a way that is understandable and easy to follow. It's a book worth reading if you are struggling with giving up the worksheets, or like me, feeling guilty about not teaching grammar.

A Grammar Lesson

Let me end my discussion of teaching grammar in context with an example of what I consider to be a grammar lesson. It can be adapted to any piece of literature, any level of students, and any form of grammar. It also fits in with any type of writing you and your students may be working on at the time. The purpose of the activity is to help students experiment with more complex sentence structures, or depending on what your students need, simply correct sentence structures. Take a look.

Mimicking the Pros

- Pull an interesting paragraph from a piece of literature the class is studying.
- Have students read the paragraph carefully in small groups and answer the following questions:
  1. What is the most interesting thing you see in this paragraph? (Consider the way a word is used, the way a sentence is constructed, and so on.)

  2. What effect does the item you've picked have on the reader?

  3. Is this something the author does often? (You may consult your text if necessary.) Explain why he or she may or may not.

  4. Try to mimic the technique in something a member of your group is writing right now. Have a group member write the finished product on an overhead sheet to share, along with what he or she had written before this revision.

- Have groups report findings. The teacher may or may not want to comment on the correct terms for the constructions students have found. It is not always necessary for students to know terms.
- Make repetitions or differences in examples a point of discussion.
- Make "why's" a point of discussion.
- Make effectiveness of before and after writings a point of discussion.

I tutored a high school student once who was convinced that through some weird circumstance she had forgotten how to write. She loved writing in elementary school, but was "a hopeless mess" now that she was in high school. Reading her work, I noticed short, very elementary sentences. We worked through some of her other writing issues, and then she read Amy Tan's *Bonesetter's Daughter* (2001). She fell in love with Tan's style and language. We worked with the paragraph that you see here:

> The following August, rather than just wait for muteness to strike, Ruth explained to her clients and friends that she was taking a planned weeklong retreat into verbal silence. "It's a yearly ritual," she said, "to sharpen my consciousness about words and their necessity." One of her book clients, a New Age psychotherapist, saw voluntary silence as a "wonderful process," and decided he would engage in the same so they could include their findings in a chapter on either dysfunctional family dynamics or stillness as therapy. (Tan, 2001)

We did not discuss terms at all. We simply looked at the combinations of ideas in Tan's sentences. As my student mimicked the sentence structure that Tan was using, she fell in love with her *own* writing, and her confidence soared. Her writing improved dramatically because she had found a way to put what was in her head on paper.

A Word of Caution

Let me add one word of caution here. Students' mistakes often increase as they try out new grammatical forms and structures in their writing. Be patient and gentle with such mistakes, and they will disappear as the writers come to better understand the new constructions. Mistakes mean that students are taking risks and learning!

For Further Ideas . . .

Constance Weaver has written another book that I encourage any one who is interested in teaching meaningful grammar in their classroom to read, *Lessons to Share on Teaching Grammar in Context* (1997). It is packed with ideas from wonderful teachers about how to approach grammar issues in a meaningful way. The most important thing, as with teaching any other writing concept, is to study your students, figure out what they need and what works for them. If something is not useful, don't continue to do it. And remember *why* you are teaching grammar: not simply for grammar's sake, but in order to improve writing.

A WORD ABOUT STANDARDS

All of this meeting students where they are and teaching grammar in context is great ideally. "But what of standards?" you ask. I certainly have standards for my students, as does Tom Romano (1987). We expect and require that they write, and write often. We insist that they work hard and work to make progress. Students who slack off, refuse to write, or refuse to take their own writing and growth as a writer seriously will not do well. Many of my high school students had much to say about my standards in their year-end reflections.

I came into the year with the idea that English was a "cake" class and an easy "A," boy was I proven wrong!

I guess what I'm trying to say is that this class gave me the challenge of my life. I would have never gotten to this level of writing if it weren't for the things I learned in this class.

I also have worked hard on my writing and have improved. . . . You've been probably the most difficult English teacher I've ever had, but the experience has been wonderful.

> This year has been a roller coaster ride from beginning to end; the class jammed the accelerator to the floor on the first day and kept it there till about a day ago when it came to a screeching halt leaving the entire class gasping. It was a blast!

Reading the students' comments, I felt I had accomplished my goal. Together, we had created a challenging class where students learned. Giving students what they need does not mean letting them take the easy way out or giving every student an A on every assignment.

If a teacher is to know whether or not a student is working hard and growing, he or she must know the student and that student's work intimately. They must watch that student write over time, and they must peruse the student's collected works thoughtfully. Sure, a student could fake me out on one or two assignments, but an intimate knowledge of the student's work makes "playing possum" very difficult over a period of time. To simply place a grade at the top of a paper based on how many mistakes in English grammar a student makes is much easier, but much less productive. At the same time, allowing students to turn in one draft of a paper, get a grade, and stuff it in their book bags to be forever forgotten requires much less of them than the multiple drafts and reflection that I am asking for. If students are going to grow as writers, they must have an intimate knowledge of their work as well.

WATCHING THE RACE: EVALUATING STUDENT WRITING

Grading Practice Writing Without Eradicating Its Purpose

There is much more to a student's writing than published or finished pieces. As a matter of fact, in my class the majority of student writing is the practice writing contained in their daybooks. Tom Romano (1987) counts these entries for a grade. He just wants to be sure that his students are practicing each day. Because of the variety of writing tasks offered in his class, he has plenty of other opportunities to read over and respond to student writing. In his class, the daybook (he calls it a "journal") is a private place for private writing and development. To grade it on content would be to sully that privacy (p. 14).

I do not feel that there is one right way to grade daybooks, or journals, or writers' notebooks, or whatever you choose to call them. I also do not grade them the same way each time. It all depends on my purpose in grading that day. Some days I may be more concerned about the students' understanding of the piece of literature they are responding to. Other days I may be happy with the fact that they are putting pen to paper in a meaningful way, and some days I'm simply happy that they put pen to paper period! I have asked many of the teachers I know who use daily writings in their classrooms how they grade them and have compiled a list of possibilities. My suggestion is to pick a method that best suits you and your students and go with it.

Grading Response Journals or Daybooks

1. Count entries.

2. Check for and read five random entries.

3. Allow students to mark entries they would like you to read.

4. Require students to write a reflection about their reading journal.

5. Randomly spot check a few journals each week.

6. Have students turn in journals on a rotating schedule.

7. Walk around and check during the last 3 minutes of writing time.

8. Give students a grade based on their responses in class from reading journals.

9. Grade for participation—if they are writing something during the allotted time, they get 100.

10. Have students include five entries in a portfolio of their best work at the end of the quarter and explain why they consider them to be the best.

11. Require students to submit journal entries that are used with a larger assignment.

If you mix and match these methods in a way that is appropriate for your students and your classroom, students will know the importance of the daybook while still feeling free to practice and experiment with it. Additionally, you as a teacher will feel less overwhelmed by the masses of student writing that you need to read and respond to.

Grading Published Pieces

Grading a completed piece of writing has as many facets and steps as the piece of writing itself. It is hypocritical to ask a student to go through the rigors of using a real process with their writing and then simply slap a grade on the top of the paper. How do they know what the grade stands for? Where were their weaknesses? Where were their triumphs? A 94 with "Nice work" written beside it does no more to help the author grow as a writer than a 69 with "Needs major improvement" scrawled beside it. Yet, we as teachers are pressed for time. We want our students to write often and get feedback often, so we must give that feedback in the most efficient way possible. I use three basic tools to help me give personalized, helpful feedback without taking hours per paper:

1. Rubrics

2. Reflective letters

3. The grammar sheet

Rubrics

Teachers need to develop grading rubrics that reflect what they want students to accomplish in their writing. A rubric should take into account everything that the teacher is looking for as she reads the paper. Students need to see how process, mechanics, organization, audience and purpose, and so on factor into their grade. Rubrics differ from teacher to teacher and from assignment to assignment.

Not only does a rubric help students know what they need to do, but it makes grading simpler for me. When we as teachers grade papers, there are certainly criteria in our heads that we are looking for. Having it in front of me in black and white helps me to be fair and give each paper equal attention. I award points for each section, noting information I think the student might need about that section to the side, add the points, and I'm done. The student knows where the grade comes from, and if there are still questions, I can see what I was thinking at the time from the notes on the rubric.

I use the following rubric when my students write literary essays. I love these assignments because students are allowed to pick their own topics. The only requirement is that the paper covers a work or works of literature that we've read during the year. Students receive the rubric with the assignment.

Literature Piece

_____ (5) Thesis

_____ (10) Organization

_____ (15) Depth of analysis

_____ (10) Support

_____ (20) Evidence of serious revision

_____ (30) Craft—reasons for choices in the following
  – Word choice
  – Sentence structure
  – Audience

_____ (10) Editing/Grammar

_____ Total Points

Notice that the rubric addresses what we would be looking for in a literature essay but also awards points for process. My students are always required to turn in all prewriting, drafts, and false starts for each paper that reaches publication. Not only have I seen what they have been doing because of in-class writing and writing workshops, but I also have a record of that work. As students come to realize that process is a part of their grade, they take it more seriously, and as they take it more seriously, they come to see the value in it. In upper-level classes where process has become more natural to students, I may tweak the rubric you see to look more like the following:

Literature Piece

_____ (5) Thesis

_____ (10) Organization

_____ (25) Depth of analysis

_____ (20) Support

_____ (30) Craft—reasons for choices in the following
–Word choice
–Sentence structure
–Audience

_____ (10) Editing/Grammar

_____ Total Points

Here, I have stepped up my expectations for writing about literature. Students are not rewarded so much for the act of revision, but I will not grade a paper that does not include the drafts and revision that I have always required. Some classes never move to this rubric, some move beyond it. Please do not feel that all rubrics must be balanced just like the one you see here. The rubric needs to fit not only the assignment, but also the students and what they need to focus on.

Rubrics and State Assessments

If you have an assessment of some sort that you and your students are working toward, you can play around with your rubrics to help students build those skills without drilling. Until 2001, the North Carolina tenth grade writing test was set up on a 6-point scale. Knowing that my students would be assessed in this way, I began to develop rubrics for writing assignments that reflected the North Carolina standards. The following rubric was for a creative piece that my students wrote when we were trying to get a handle on the concept of theme. Compare it to the rubric my students received for end-of-course practice essays.

THEME PAPER

Scoring Rubric

_____ 0

    _____ Does not have a theme

_____ 1

    _____ Has a very vague theme

_____ 2

    _____ Addresses the theme a little
    _____ Difficulty focusing on topic
    _____ Overall poor organization

_____ 3

    _____ Addresses the theme almost throughout the piece
    _____ Focuses on one topic
    _____ Uses conventions of the English language properly

_____ 4

    _____ Addresses the theme throughout the piece
    _____ Has some transitions between points
    _____ Few mistakes in spelling or grammar

_____ 5

    _____ Addresses the theme throughout the piece
    _____ Has strong transitions between points/no break in the progression of ideas
    _____ Uses large vocabulary skillfully
    _____ Sentence structure is varied and effective
    _____ There is a strong sense of audience
    _____ Effective approach to the theme (tone, point of view, and originality)
    _____ Clear evidence of revision from free write to final paper
    _____ No mistakes in spelling or grammar

_____ 6

    _____ Everything is present from score point 5

EOC ESSAY SCORING RUBRIC

_____ 0

     _____ Does not address the prompt

_____ 1

     _____ Plot summary
     _____ Only addresses part of the prompt

_____ 2

     _____ Addresses the prompt
     _____ Plot summary
     _____ Lists/Little commentary
     _____ Weak supporting details

_____ 3

     _____ Addresses all aspects of the prompt
     _____ Very little plot summary
     _____ Very little listing
     _____ Supporting details
     _____ Commentary present

_____ 4

     _____ Addresses all aspects of the prompt
     _____ Has some transitions between points
     _____ No plot summary
     _____ No lists
     _____ Strong supporting details
     _____ Strong commentary
     _____ Few mistakes in spelling or grammar

_____ 5

     _____ Addresses all aspects of the prompt
     _____ Has strong transitions between points/no break in the progression of ideas
     _____ Specific details clearly link events and relationships
     _____ Uses large vocabulary skillfully
     _____ Sentence structure is varied and effective
     _____ There is a strong sense of audience

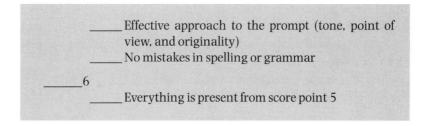

_____ Effective approach to the prompt (tone, point of view, and originality)
_____ No mistakes in spelling or grammar

_____ 6

_____ Everything is present from score point 5

I simply replaced the idea of addressing the prompt with what we were focusing on in our study at the moment, maintaining a theme. I developed both rubrics in order to help my students see the "real writing" aspects of the state exam. Sadly, process was not, and still is not, a factor in the test; therefore you do not see anything pertaining to process in these rubrics. For these assignments, process was a separate grade and a separate rubric. I have also developed rubrics for various assignments using AP and IB grading criteria. I have listed some other excellent examples from other published professionals in the Suggested Reading at the end of this chapter. I encourage you to take a look and develop your own rubrics to fit the need of your classrooms.

The Reflective Letter

The writing conferences discussed in Chapter 7 will help you know what's going on with your student's writing, but another great tool is a reflective letter. At the bottom of each rubric I hand out, there is always a note about the letter I expect to receive. The letter assignment is keyed to the writing assignment. The letter for the literature paper rubric looked like this:

Letter:
Process of writing the piece
What you want your reader to see in the piece
Evidence of craft—your reasoning behind these decisions
Anything else you would like to tell me

I have my students attach a letter with each piece of writing that is to be graded. Here they tell me the process they went through in writing the piece, what they were trying to do, what they are particularly proud of, and what they are concerned about. By reading these letters, I have a window into the writer's mind and thereby the written piece before I even begin reading it. It takes the guesswork out of evaluation for me. By reading the letter, I can evaluate not only the words on the page, but the thinking process that went into the writing.

The following is a sample of one of the letters I received with the literature piece assignment.

Mrs. U:

For this piece, I planned, in rough, what I wanted the paper to convey. I wanted a new look at how the motivations in *Siddhartha* and *Les Miserables* compared and contrasted. When I actually sat down to write the piece, I let my imagination run free. My plan was my only guide, providing the centering upon which my magnificent diagonals were constructed.

In this work, I hope to give the reader a new way to look at comparative essay. Instead of a formulaic, predictable straightforward piece, I wanted to stimulate the reader's mind. I want them to think about what they're reading, and I want them to be able to still have room to form their own conclusions, instead of having everything placed in front of them as absolute fact. In a way, they're interpreting my interpretation of the comparison of the motivations and actions in *Les Miserables*. I believe that my main influence for this work would be the writing test which we were forced to complete earlier this year. After months of guided and straight writing which caused everyone's work to sound almost the same, I had to branch off. I decided to write, not in a way where you had to state your intent in the first, third and fifteenth-and-a-half line, but in a way that after the work was read, the intent was what the reader made of it. This paper is, in a way, a combination of how Hugo represented his country, and how Hesse represented the human spirit. Nothing is stated forthright, nothing is wrong, but in the same way nothing is right. I am quite frankly unsure about this piece. I don't know how others will be able to deal with it. I know that the last work of this nature did go over well with you, but the subject of that page was far less serious. I know that, in my mind, this paper works in all of the ways that it should.

The paper attached to this letter was one that would have made me say, "What in the world was this kid thinking?" The letter answered the question and forced me to take a closer look at what the student was attempting to do. My student actually *had* met his goals, but they were his goals, not mine, and I would have missed that fact without the letter.

The young lady who wrote the following letter struggled with her writing at the beginning of the year. Had I not read her letter before grading the written piece, I probably would have picked up on how important the piece is to her, but not to the extent that I did after reading the letter. I also was able to tell how much thought and work she had put into it.

Mrs. Urbanski—

For my personal piece I decided to do something very personal. It's a story of a very triumphant part of my life that I am very proud of. I've always wanted to write something about it just so I could look back on it when I'm older, and as a sort of tribute to the people that helped make this story with a happy ending. I wrote this with all of my personal views, feelings, and memories to try to take the reader into the same position that I was in. I used first person to help the reader get a better feeling of the experiences through my point of view. I've written this piece intending everyone to read it and get something out of it. Shy people can read this to help them see that they're not alone, to give them hope that they can defeat this illness, and to help them to solve their problems. By reading this, others can also take a walk in the world of a shy person, which will enable them to better understand just how difficult this type of thing can be. Perhaps it will solve a little confusion they might be having as to why some people act the way they do. Perhaps with this piece, people can reach out and try to help the shy people conquer their fears. In this piece I used experiences or examples from my own life. I used these so the reader can step into my shoes to feel the things I went through and hear my inner thoughts. I start from the present, and then take a sort of flashback to the stages leading up to now. I like the way I tied it all together at the end by bringing the reader back to the present. I think it makes the piece seem more complete and concludes the missing link from the introduction. Overall, I am glad that I was given this assignment because it enabled me to write something I never got around to writing and say thanks to these people that mean so much to me. Writing this also brought me back to those days and made me feel a new sense of pride for what I did. It touched me when I saw the tears running down my mother's face after she had read it. What do these tears mean? Mission accomplished. Thanks Mrs. Urbanski.

Reading the letter informs me of the huge amount of effort the student put into creating a piece of writing that she is proud of. She has a definite audience and a specific purpose. I know that in order to encourage her to continue writing, I need to acknowledge and praise her effort because it is genuine. It also lets me know that any mistakes I find are not simply carelessness, but present a real learning opportunity.

The letters are also a good gauge for whether or not I am accomplishing my goals as a teacher. These two letters show me that I am building trust and helping my students create writing that is meaningful to them. On a less positive note, in the first letter I found that, although I thought I was keeping the state writing test from taking over my classroom, I hadn't quite succeeded. That letter inspired me to let the test go during the pilot year that I described in Chapter 2.

Reflection letters are valuable tools for both the writer and the teacher. It forces the writer to look closely at their own process and gives teachers a glimpse into the student's mind.

The Grammar Sheet

The most valuable tool I have for working with grammar errors in students' papers is what my students and I call the "grammar sheet." It stays in the back of their daybooks, and they add to it as they need it. The purpose of this handy little tool is to help students identify and work with the grammar mistakes they make and to keep teachers from fruitlessly marking the same mistakes over and over again on student papers.

Here's how it works.

- Mark a particular mistake up to three times on the student's paper.

- Have students use group members, handbooks, and teacher if necessary to define the mistake.
- Have students correct the mistakes you have marked as well as the others that may exist in the paper.
- Have students write down the rule in their own words, along with an example on the grammar sheet in back of the daybook.
- Have students ask peer editors to look for the mistake in the next paper.
- Have students attach a note to the next paper reminding you of the mistakes they have been working with.
- Make a tick mark in the margin of the paper if the noted mistake occurs again.
- Repeat the process until the mistake is mostly eradicated. Add other issues when the student seems ready.
- Students consult their grammar sheets each time they go through the editing process.

The grammar sheet makes up the major part of my grammar instruction. It allows the students to keep up with their own personal trouble spots and work through those systematically. Working in the UNC-Charlotte Writing Resources Center, I found that most people make only about three mistakes; they just make them chronically. If I can help the students pinpoint those mistakes and clear them up, then I've done something major for them in terms of grammar instruction.

Using the three tools I have mentioned, I can read and respond to student writing in an efficient manner. My students and I are able to understand each other's expectations, and I am able to help students grow as writers.

PORTFOLIOS: LOOKING AT THE WHOLE SEASON AND STUDENT GROWTH OVER TIME

My students turn in a portfolio at the end of each semester that is worth anywhere from 50 percent to 100 percent of their grade. As I alluded to earlier, each student has a writing folder that contains all writing, including drafts, false starts, and unfinished pieces.

When the time comes to assign a semester grade, I spend a good deal of time reviewing these folders and thinking about each student's growth. Portfolios are collections of several pieces the students choose to represent their best work and growth. I am continually playing with the arrangement of the portfolio and the types of assignments that my students are required to highlight, but here is the latest one. My hope is that it represents their growth as writers in each phase of the writing process.

Semester Portfolio

1. A reflective essay thoroughly explaining the reasoning behind the choices you have made for this portfolio. How do they signify you as a writer and a reader and the progress you have made this year? What grade do you think you should be awarded, and what do you base it on? What areas of your writing do you want to focus on in the future, and how can your classmates and I help you do that?

2. Six daybook entries
    1 reader response
    1 reflection letter from a paper carried through the writing process
    1 free write that eventually became a published piece
    2 of your own choice

3. Three published or graded pieces, including all drafts and planning
    1 literature-based topic
    2 of your choice

4. Two pieces that you would like to revise
    (These do not have to have been published, but they certainly may have been.)

5. Anything else that you would like to include from this class or any other experience in or out of school that will show your development as a writer

6. A list of three grammar or usage mistakes that you have identified as trouble spots in your writing, along with a description of how you recognize them and what you do to correct them

The portfolio is such an important part of my students' grade because it gives them an opportunity to show me what they consider to be their best work and tell me why. It takes the responsibility for being the complete judge and jury of their writing off me, and it forces them to think about their own progress and growth. Because the students pick what goes in the portfolio, they are allowed to have bad writing days, and weeks. A certain idea or topic that just was not working for them for whatever reason will not completely decimate their grade for the semester. The portfolio treats students as real writers who have ups and downs, good days and bad, and can make choices about what they want to be remembered by or evaluated for.

The most important part of the portfolio is the reflection letter. Without it, the portfolio would simply be a notebook check and a grade for organization. Students are much more careful about the things they pick for their portfolios if they must explain those choices. Similar to the reflective letters that I require for each published paper, the portfolio letters also give me a window into my students' minds. After I have read the letters, I do not have to reread every paper in the portfolio, though I can never stop myself from flipping through them. The growth of the writer and the thought behind the construction of the portfolio usually becomes quite clear after I have read what they have to say about it. Also, as students write these letters, they always notice things that they had forgotten from earlier in the year.

Portfolios count for a big part of the grade because I am not nearly as interested in the performance of a student on a single assignment as I am in growth over time. The portfolio grade allows me to grade my students and what they consider to be their best work and their progress—two things that are a must if we are going to help students grow as writers and encourage them to write more.

CONCLUSIONS

A grade should be a reflection of a student's learning, not a weapon or bribe to force her to work. We should not become involved in the task of counting mistakes in order to justify a grade, but rather encouraging and nurturing students in a way that will make them want to become better writers. Requiring students to work hard, think, and grow as writers each day is much more rigorous for all involved than simply requiring papers that are formatted perfectly but in the end have little to say. We need to act as coaches, cheering our students on to victory and noting the things that are holding them back, so that we can help them overcome those obstacles in the next race.

SUGGESTED READING

Clark, Roy Peter. (1987). *Free to write: A journalist teaches young writers.* Portsmouth, NH: Heinemann.
Romano, Tom. (1987). *Clearing the way: Working with teenage writers.* Portsmouth, NH: Heinemann.

CHAPTER SEVEN

Responding as a Spectator

The Writing Conference

W hen I was working on my master's degree and took an assistantship with the English department that placed me as a tutor in the Writing Resources Center (WRC) at UNC-Charlotte, I felt prepared to handle any writing problem that was presented to me. I thought I knew how to talk to students about their writing. I even resented having to go to training. Come on, I was a teacher, I worked with high school students, I knew exactly what I was doing.

But then Sue Diehl, our director, began to talk about tutoring. "We sit side by side," she said. Okay, no problem, I usually do that with my students; it makes them more comfortable. "We share the paper," she said. Okay, a little inconvenient, but I can deal with that. I don't mind making the writer feel the ownership of the paper. "And we never, never write on papers." *Panic!* How was I going to help students without writing on their papers? How was I going to remember what was wrong with the paper when they read it out loud to me?

Finally she told us, "We instruct, through questions; we try *very* hard not to *tell* the students what to do, but to help them find solutions to the problems that they see or feel in the paper."

"Well," I thought, "this woman is certainly nuts. How will they know if they have problems with something? Wouldn't they

121

fix them on their own if they knew they had them?" Still, these were the rules, and I had to admit that I was intrigued. It would be great to give students that much power over their own writing . . . if it really worked.

In my first few days as a tutor in the writing center, I discovered that if I concentrated on focus and organization, I could find plenty "wrong" with the papers. I had plenty to talk about without even dealing with proofreading issues. I was feeling pretty successful as I pointed out to students where their papers lost focus, or how their thoughts should be organized, and then encouraged them to come back to work with chronic grammar problems. Ah, how wonderful it would be to have 50 minutes to show my high school students what they were doing wrong!

Then toward the end of the third week, I had an epiphany. The classes *I* was taking were in full swing, and I had been up most of the night finishing a paper. I had tutored for 6 hours straight that day, and I was exhausted. A student came in with an eight-page engineering paper and began to read it to me. I struggled to pay attention and follow along, but much to my dismay, I discovered when he came to the end that my mind had been wandering. I panicked. I had nothing to say. I put on my best Socratic face and said, "Well, how do you see this paper right now?" I waited in despair for the student to expose my fraud, but instead he said, "I'm having trouble with organization, my information is all over the place, and I don't know what passive voice is."

"Hey!" I thought. "This questioning thing might work!" I decided to keep trying. "Show me where you think the organization is weak."

"Well, like right here."

"Cool," I thought. "We can do this."

I had no agenda of my own for the paper, and it changed the tone of the session. I had to depend on the student to answer my questions, and I couldn't fish for the answer I wanted because I had no earthly idea what that might be! I was no longer dictating the direction of the session, but letting the student identify his own concerns and then deal with them.

We organized his thoughts by making a list of all the topics he was covering, assigning each a color, and then color-coding the paper according to the key we had made. The color-coding, or "rainbow organization" as I like to call it, was my only contribution. He made all of the decisions about what points he was tying to make and what things went together. I just sat back and watched.

Satisfied with the organization, we moved to passive voice. Though I was much more familiar with his paper by now, I decided to keep going with my questioning.

"What do you think passive voice is? Can you show me where you think you've used it?"

He showed me a sentence, and he was right.

"Good! Now show me where you haven't used it."

Right again!

"What's the difference between those two?"

Bingo! He figured it out.

The student left the center grinning from ear to ear. "Thanks so much, I know what I need to do."

He returned a few weeks later to show me the A on his paper. He thanked me again, and I was able to say with absolute sincerity for the first time, "Don't thank me, you did all of the work!"

Hair-raising though the experience was for me, I learned that my fundamental mistake in conferencing with students was in hunting for their mistakes. If I just shut up and listened to the students, they would be able to take me where they needed to go.

It worked! My students in the WRC began to answer all of my questions and find their own difficulties. Many times, if I would just sit, listen, and repeat what they said, they would do all of the work themselves. At the end of sessions, they would look at me with surprise and say, "I really feel much better about this, thank you." To which I would reply with a smile, "But you did all of the work."

Through tutoring, I began to understand the writing conference, see the absolute necessity in it, and see the kinds of lessons we could teach student writers using it. I have always made a habit of walking around when my students were working on a piece of writing and answering any questions they might have. That is certainly a form of conferencing. As I began to read more about conferencing and think more about the types of conversations that I had with my students, I began to see how much of what I was doing in the WRC could really be carried over to my classroom.

WHY CONFERENCE ANYWAY?

Why in the world, especially in a high school classroom, should we take the time to conference with each individual on a regular basis? It's going to take up tremendous amounts of time that we could be using to teach literature, and loads of patience and organization to set it up. Since all students make pretty much the same mistakes at one time or another, why don't we just say it one time instead of 100?

But then think for a moment. How many times have you been involved in a wonderful lesson on writing, excitedly talking away only to notice that the one person who really needed to hear what you are saying most is looking at you with that "Is she ever going to shut up?" expression. You may go over and tap their desk, ask them a question, anything to get them into what you are saying, but the minute you leave their side they go adrift again.

Our first thought is that the student is simply ignoring us and doesn't care about learning to write. Some would even take it as far as to say, "His loss." But what if there is another reason? What if the student simply does not understand or see the relevance of what you are saying in relationship to what he is writing? Yes, he is aware that he has problems with writing. All of his papers come back dripping red ink. But he doesn't see the relationship between what you are saying and the marks. Also, he has decided that he is a horrible writer anyway, so there is no point in trying any more.

To me, the number one reason to conference with students is that we want them to see themselves as writers. For many of our high school students, seeing themselves as writers necessitates breaking through years of being told that they are not. One of my students summed up what I'm trying to say here beautifully in her end-of-year reflection:

> I'm terrible at writing. When I was younger I could maybe write the one or two odd school newspaper articles but nothing that would be graded, forget it. The teacher should have given me a negative 10% and moved on, that was how terrible and underdeveloped my writing was. As these thoughts entered my head I remembered my English teacher saying that if we didn't consider ourselves writers now (at the beginning of the school year) that she hoped we would consider

ourselves writers at the end of the school year. I rolled my eyes to that comment, thinking, "Yah, right, sure lady, me a writer." To my surprise, my English teacher was right. . . . I cannot believe the improvement I've made in the past nine months and I actually may come to regard myself as a writer.

This young lady was in the International Baccalaureate program at our school, one of the best and brightest. Still, she entered her sophomore year convinced she would never be a writer. What a change that year brought!

Because we are not working with students as individuals and getting to know their writing and writing processes, we are sending students to college who are quite convinced they will never be writers. For instance, at the beginning of the spring semester, a young woman came into the writing center, declaring her inability to write. She had to write one paper for a history class on Toni Morrison's *Beloved* (1987) and how it reflected the lives of slaves shortly after the Emancipation Proclamation. My first thought was, "Well, this book is complicated, no wonder she's struggling; she probably doesn't understand it."

But then she began to talk to me about her paper. She showed me a rough outline and then pages and pages of handwritten drafts with words, lines, and entire paragraphs crossed out. The margins were riddled with notes and arrows. It was a wonderful, delightful, mess. Then she had about 10 typed pages that also were beginning to show the signs of deep thinking and revision. Still, she was so embarrassed about her writing that she wouldn't let me read it. She preferred to tell me what she had done.

As she discussed the novel and its relevance to the Reconstruction Period in U.S. history, I began to see that she had a wonderful understanding of the book, all of its intricacies and symbols, and more important for the paper she was writing, the novel's significance to history.

In my notes on this session I wrote:

_____ is a very intelligent young woman. She breezed through *Beloved* very quickly and has a very deep understanding of the novel. The problem, in her words, is that "She is a horrible writer." She wouldn't even let me read what she had written. (Jan. 26, 2000)

After I questioned her a little more about what she had been writing, she said that she felt like her thoughts were really unorganized and she didn't know what to do about that. She was absolutely disgusted with everything she had written and wanted to throw it away and start over, but she was afraid that would be even worse.

Before addressing her concern about organization, I asked her why she was such a horrible writer. In my notes, I paraphrased her response as:

> After a lot of questioning, _____ admitted that she felt herself to be a poor writer because she missed the basics in a bad school until the 8th grade. (Jan. 26, 2000)

This wonderfully intelligent young woman, who had such a feel for the English language that she understood *Beloved* on the first read, believed that she couldn't write because her grammar was less than perfect.

As I questioned her more, I found that her real issue with what she had written was that it did not really represent her thoughts. She was self-editing so much as she wrote that she couldn't think.

She came back to the writing center five times for the same paper. Each time, her confidence grew. Most of what we did for her was fawn over how much she had to say. I wish I could count the number of times I said, "Write down what you just said; it was brilliant." We gave her a few tricks to get the words out, and she ran with them. About two weeks later, she came back into the center with tears in her eyes saying, "I got an A! I've never gotten an A. This is probably the last paper I'll ever really have to write and I'm really disappointed about that now. I can't believe I got an A."

Now consider a different scenario. Suppose this student never came into the writing center, but sat at home struggling through her multiple drafts. She turns in the final paper, riddled with mistakes, and very simplistic language. Based on the final draft alone, the teacher decides that the paper was obviously thrown together at the last minute, marks up all the mistakes, grades down for lack of thoughtfulness, and returns it to the student, maybe with a cursory comment on taking more time with assignments. Our student would have celebrated the fact that she would never have to write another college paper and taken the grade and comments as solid evidence that she could not write.

Here we have another reason for conferencing. If we talk with our students about their writing, then we can see the paper through their eyes. We can find out what they have been doing and help them. Without the benefit of this talk, evaluating writing becomes a guessing game.

Let me give you an even more glaring example of how a student's talk about his writing can tell a teacher why he wrote something in the way that he did. Another wonderful student came into the writing center. He was a very serious young man who followed me over to the center after a presentation I did for the chemistry department. He made an appointment and then followed me down to the drink machines to talk. He matter-of-factly stated that he was a transfer student and therefore in a freshman writing class that he felt was beneath him. He felt himself to be a very good writer, but his teacher did not share his opinion of his work. He was angry and frustrated and wanted a second opinion. I was very surprised when I found out exactly who his professor was. She is a wonderful teacher and is generally loved by all of her students. I decided that there must be something wrong with this guy. Still, I smiled and assured him that I thought we could help him.

When he came in and began to read his paper, I was struck by his wonderful skill. The writing was absolutely poetic. The assignment was to pick five items that described your culture and the culture of the year 2000 to place in a time capsule and then explain their significance. This student, a chemistry major oddly enough, had picked several pieces of literature, including *Hamlet, Henry V, The Brothers Karamozoff,* the Bible, and *1984.* His sentence structure was wonderfully varied and his vocabulary extensive. But the paper was terribly underdeveloped.

He did explain a little about why he chose each work, but said nothing about how that work fit with the criteria of the choice. I asked what he thought about the teacher's comment about the development of the piece. His response was, "Of course it's underdeveloped, she said three to five pages, this is all I had *room* to write."

Bingo! He *knew* what to do. He had simply misunderstood directions. I knew that his professor did not really care about the number of pages and had only said that to give her students a general idea of what to do. I encouraged him to fully develop his thoughts, and he revised the paper into a truly beautiful piece.

We can only find out why our students make the writing choices they make by *listening* to them. As we come to understand these choices, bizarre though they may seem to us, the more we can help our students grow as writers.

Donald Graves (1991) lists three reasons for conferencing with our students about their writing:

1. When the child talks, we learn.

2. When the child talks, the child learns.

3. When the child talks, the teacher can help. (p. 137)

Giving students time to talk with us about their writing takes a lot of the guesswork out of writing instruction. Often, we will learn something about the student's process or concepts of writing that we did not know before, as in the case of the student I just discussed. Other times, a student will come to see that she knows more about a subject than it seemed that she did before, as in the case of the young woman working with *Beloved.* And finally, we can address the problems that students are struggling with, according to the students, instead of guessing and lecturing on something that may not seem relevant to that student in that moment.

We are also giving our students a forum to talk about their writing in a way that real writers do. Peter Elbow (1973) talks about the phenomenon that occurs for the writer who has someone to share her work with in different stages on a regular basis. Elbow feels that sharing makes writing easier because it allows the writer to know how people react to her words. He compares writing alone with the uncomfortable situation of talking to a stranger.

> He is hard to "read." He might have very different responses from those you are used to. When you get *no* clues, speaking is especially difficult. . . .
>
> In writing, however, this is the normal condition. No wonder it is agony. As you are writing you get no clues as to how readers will react. You have to write the whole thing out, keep going till the end, even though you have no idea whether the reader is lost or thinks you are crazy at the end of the first paragraph. (Elbow, 1973, p. 124)

The fact that Elbow is speaking here of an adult writing class without teachers makes his words even more applicable to our students. As has been the theme throughout this book, if we want our students to become writers, then we must treat them as such. Real people who wish to become real writers need someone to listen to their writing. They need reactions so that they might see how their words are working. In our classrooms, we are the most qualified, especially in the beginning, to be that sounding board, not because we are teachers looking for error, but because we are good readers, practiced at making meaning from a written text.

A TREK THROUGH A CONFERENCE LOG

As I began to think about a chapter on conferencing, I spent about an hour one Saturday morning looking through my WRC conference log to see what types of issues come up when I talk with students about their writing. I was surprised at how many there were. As a teacher, I worried that time I took to conference with individual students would take away from my instructional time— time I had to *teach things.* Looking through my notes, I found that my students provided me with plenty of topics. When I was teaching at the high school level, I would spend hours trying to think of ways to teach "writing" in ways that would catch my students' attention. There was no planning time involved in any of the situations described following, in excerpts from my conference log. I saw each paper for the first time when the student sat down with me to work. It is amazing what I have covered with them and what they have come to understand because the conferences were directed toward their concerns.

Writing Conventions/Skills in Context

Transitions

_____ has made tremendous progress with her paper, but she is concerned that there are no connections between her ideas. We worked to build a transition between the first two topics, and she was able to do the rest on her own. (Jan. 31, 2000)

Coherence

We did have one major breakthrough today when we were working from an old scholarship letter. It was only a page and a half long, so he could see how very disconnected it was. I talked to him a little about coherence and pointed out how we were trying to make all of the ideas connect through out the essay. He handed me a pen so that I could write what I had just said down for him—this tells me that he understands, sees the value of it and wants to remember it. (Jan. 26, 2000)

Using Quotes in a Literary Critique

He has a better understanding of how to incorporate literature into a paper. It was interesting to me how easy it was to explain this when I got him to think of the way his audience may interpret the quotes by giving him an interpretation that I knew was not his point. He saw that in order to get his point across he needed to explain his own interpretation. (March 14, 2000).

Finding a Focus

As _____ explained the books she was using for this paper, she found a neat focus of using children's literature in a multidisciplinary unit with science. (May 1, 2000)

_____ is writing a claim of policy. His claim was that there needed to be more deer management. But when he defined that term, he found that there were many more aspects to deer management than the hunting limits that he was covering in his paper. As I asked him about the other aspects, he found that he didn't want to address all of those issues, so he changed his focus. (May 2, 2000)

A Look at Conventions Taught/Discussed Over a Series of Conferences

He expressed some frustration with the fact that we were "wasting" the last 20 minutes of our sessions. I assured him that from what I had seen our conversation was very productive. For the next session, I think I will begin with a review of everything he has learned from what I have seen as this draft develops:

Center of Gravity—Focus
Audience
Purpose
Vision
Process—Finding his own
Invention
Expansion
His writing shows that he has mastered all of these.
(Feb. 28, 2000)

Tips in Context

_____ felt that her writing did not represent her ideas and when it did, it was really unorganized. I suggested free writing all of her ideas and then going back and organizing them by color-coding the different ideas in her paper and then matching like colors. As I wrote these tips down, she seemed very excited to try them. (Jan. 26, 2000)

Discovering the Real Reasons for Problems in a Piece

She did a much better job relating her experience as an exchange student to her life in the world of international business. She still is having a problem directly stating what she wants to say. I questioned her about this in on one particular instance and she stated that she was afraid of coming on too strong. It seems that her desire not to offend is taking all meaning out of her words. (Feb. 1, 2000)

Encouragement, Another Point of View

_____ did not see the potential in his piece that I did. He was excited and charged up to write some more when I spoke about what I saw—a story of two young men and their dedication to God—their adventures because of this. He began to see it too. (Feb. 14, 2000).

As I look through my conference log, I see all of the things happening that I have tried to teach for years in my classroom. By responding to student writing as a reader rather than a teacher searching for errors, I was able to make these concepts relevant to my students. I covered the information as each student was ready to receive it. They remember and use these skills because they truly learned and applied them.

A 50-MINUTE TUTORING SESSION TRANSLATED INTO A 90-MINUTE CLASS

Looking at this subheading, some of you may feel that you know why I never became a math teacher. How in the world can I even begin to think that I could cram what I did with one student in a 50-minute tutoring session into the approximate 2 1/2 minutes I would have with each student in a 90-minute class?

I am not crazy, and though I am a little deficient in math, I do realize the time constraints we all face in the high school literature-based classroom. But by now you should have realized that I am asking all of us to restructure that classroom, to break away from the traditional lecture format. If we can do that, we will have time to conference with our students.

Please realize that each teacher has to develop her own style of conferencing. As with all of the other suggestions in the book, what you see here is only an *example* of what you can do. Please feel compelled to tweak it to fit you and your students' best interest. All I ask is that you know why you make the choices you do as you set up your conferences, and that your choices reflect your desire to give students a reader's response to their writing along with a coach's intervention.

There are many great books that talk of setting up a conference-based classroom. Donald Graves's *Writing: Teachers and Children at Work* (1996) focuses on the elementary classroom. Nancy Atwell's *In the Middle* (1987) concentrates on the middle school classroom, and Janet Allen's *It's Never Too Late* (1995) is the story of her high school students. What you are about to see is how I have combined their wonderful ideas with some of my own and those of my colleagues in order to come up with a construction that works for my classroom and my students.

We established in the previous chapter that students need extended writing periods in class. These are the periods that I use for the majority of my conferences. On a schedule where my classes meet every other day for 90 minutes, "writing day" is every third class day. This does not mean that we do not write at all on the other days, but writing is *all* we do on writing days.

There are several different conferencing opportunities in a writing day. The first, easiest, and in many ways most productive, is to walk around and talk to students as they work. The conversations can last from 15 seconds to 2 minutes, but that is plenty of time to offer encouragement ("I love the way the words work in that line"), offer a quick strategy ("Why don't you just free write in your daybook for a moment on that idea since you are stuck"), or see the progress that a student is making ("Wow, you've done a lot of work on this piece; you will want to sign up for a conference soon"). These short conversations can get students over any bumps they have encountered and spur them on in their writing. It also gives me a wonderful opportunity to monitor the progress of the class.

Another opportunity for conferencing is a group conference. Karen Haag of the UNC-Charlotte Writing Project came up with a brilliant tool for her elementary students called "the fluid revision circle." Nodghia Fesperman has perfected that idea for high school students. Students choose to come to the circle, and then the teacher works in a specific order (clockwise, counterclockwise, and so forth) with each student while the others listen and contribute to the conversation if they have something to say. I set up six chairs in a circle and let the students fill the chairs as they are ready. If all of the chairs don't fill, that's okay, but I never have more than six.

The word *fluid* alludes to the idea that students can come and go as they please. After I finish working with one student, she is free to return to her desk and write, or she may sit and listen for more ideas. Some students leave the circle without ever talking directly to me about their papers. They may hear something in another conversation that answers their question or spurs them to write. As students leave, others can join the circle. Many days, I can meet with half of my class in a 30-minute time frame. In a fluid revision circle, students can find ideas and work on larger trouble spots like overall focus and organization. They can also ask quick questions about things such as punctuation conventions or get several readers' reactions to a short passage that they are not sure about. And to me, the best part is that all of the information does not come from me. The students learn to help each other with their writing.

Students can also sign up for individual 5-minute conferences during a writing period. Because high school students tend to write longer pieces, I like for them to give me a copy of what they will be bringing the night before so that I have a chance to read it and be ready to talk about it. Tom Romano (1987) suggests taking a few short notes as you read the piece; this is a great suggestion as long as you are taking notes as an interested reader rather than a teacher hunting for error (p. 89). I like to reserve these conferences for students who have completed drafts that they would like some feedback on or who think that they are ready to publish a piece. I can handle most other things that come up in a walk-by conference or a revision circle, but if a student really feels the need to talk to me, I will not prevent him from signing up. Though I normally try to do about four of these in a writing day, I will do more or less depending on the state of the writing in the class. If many students are finishing up drafts or pieces, I may spend the entire period doing individual conferences. The key is flexibility!

Here is what the schedule for a typical writing day might look like:

10 minutes: Time for our own writing

10 minutes: Walk around conferences

20 minutes: Four 5-minute individual conferences

10 minutes: Walk around conferences

30 minutes: Fluid revision circles

10 minutes: Showcase student work

All of the time limits can be adjusted to the needs of the class except the first 10 minutes and the last 10 minutes. I need to write with my students each day, and on writing days in which I teach three classes, that gives me 30 minutes of my own writing time. The last 10 minutes are always used for showcasing a single student's work.

Sometimes students sign up for that slot; they may volunteer that day if no one has signed up; or I may ask a particular person to read something that I think should be shared. Just be sure that everyone in the class gets equal opportunity to be in the spotlight. I ask that all comments about the spotlighted work be positive. To me, this is a time to celebrate our writing accomplishments. If the piece is long, the student picks his favorite part, the part that will make the others want to check it out of the library of our works that we keep in the back of the room and read it in its entirety.

Writing days never run smoothly at the beginning of the year. It takes a few weeks for students to come to see the importance of the conversations that I am having with other students and to realize that they too will have their turn. It takes a few weeks for the students to figure out what to do with themselves if they are stuck, or finished, or confused. But slowly, with some modeling and practice, they fall into it, and by October, writing days are my favorite. The room has a low buzz as students write, or turn to one another for a quick read and opinion, or move in and out of the revision circle, or take the media center pass to do some quick research. By then they have learned that they are to write, that there are multiple resources besides *me* to answer questions that come up, that I will eventually get to them, and that if one piece of writing isn't working that day, they can always begin something new or pull something old from their folder. What fabulously productive days those are!

BASIC BEHAVIOR IN THE WRITING CONFERENCE

As I was flipping through Donald Graves's book *Writing: Teachers and Children at Work* (1996), I noticed a section on discipline in the writing conference. "Interesting," I thought. "I never really thought of having discipline problems in a writing conference; kids are usually pretty well behaved when I'm one on one with them. But who knows, with kids today anything can happen."

As I continued to read, I chuckled at myself when I found that Graves was talking about discipline for the *teacher*. He was addressing the same issues that my boss in the WRC had addressed about not taking over the student's paper—exactly what I had been doing in my own classroom. We as teachers need to continually monitor our own behavior during writing conference in order to guard against the grievous mistake of taking away a student's ownership of her writing.

The first and perhaps most simple way in which to break down the barriers of student versus teacher in the writing conference is the positioning of the chairs. The student and the teacher should be sitting side by side, at equal height, with the paper shared between them. Having the teacher look at your paper while towering over you from the vast expanse of the "teacher desk" can be intimidating to a student. Teachers who are much taller than their students may want to contrive some way to balance the height issue by using a lower chair or adjustable chairs for students.

When I walk around to work with students, I often sit on my knees on the floor beside a student's desk rather than tower over him. But this position can get very uncomfortable if the conversation becomes extensive. Pulling together student desks works well for me also.

I found that for extended conferences, a neutral area works best. Even if I pull a chair to my side of my desk for the students, they don't seem comfortable. My desk is the only personal space I have in my classroom, and I teach my students to respect that. Placing their paper on *my* desk is relinquishing control of it. They are often tense and never seem to know what to do with their arms and legs. If I move to the big table in the corner, students immediately plop down beside me, stretch their legs out comfortably, and prop their elbows on the table. The body language says it all.

The most difficult thing for me when I began working in the writing center was leaving the paper on the table between us. As I've said earlier, my natural instinct was to pick it up and examine it for error. I quickly saw the difference between the two actions. If I left the paper on the table, even the most timid students would eventually lean in as they read to me, point to things they had questions about, and point to text in response to my questions. If I picked up the paper and began to read, students would lean back in their chairs, stare out the window, and take in the conversations that were going on around us. Just picking up the paper gave students the idea that I was going to take care of everything and that they did not need to be present for the conference.

Another point of teacher discipline is letting the student do the majority of the talking. Such behavior is incredibly difficult for us teacher types. We are used to professing words of wisdom with every breath we take. Sometimes I have to sit with my hand over my mouth and force myself to listen. I usually know I'm talking too much when my student is looking at me with glazed eyes, nodding and saying "Um humm" a lot. "Um humm" usually translates, "Okay, I'm waiting for you to shut up so that I can ask the question that I *really* want to know the answer to."

Along with the idea of not talking too much comes the concept of wait-time. We've all heard of the 15 seconds we are supposed to wait when we ask our classes a question. In the writing conference, it may take even longer, especially with older students (Graves, 1996, p. 99). Through their vast experience in school they have learned that if they wait long enough, the teacher will answer the question for them. We have to wait them out; eventually they will answer. If they don't know the answer, they will tell you that as well. And in many cases, if you are asking the right questions, you don't know the answer yourself and the student *has* to answer; she is the only one that has the information.

Students also need that time to think of the response. If we are asking real questions about their writing, the answer may not be on the tip of their tongues. They need to be comfortable taking time to think about their answers to our questions if they are to learn anything from them. Letting the student keep control is a constant mental battle for many teachers. Often, we take control without even realizing that we have done it. In our excitement or frustration over a student's piece, we find that we can't help ourselves.

Looking back over transcripts of conferences and tutoring sessions, I find myself faltering over and over again. I notice things that I didn't notice in my reflections on the conference. The time-consuming work of taping and transcribing student conferences really helps me to keep myself in check. Seeing my own words on the page in relationship to the student's allows me to know who got to talk the most as well as what was being said in that conversation. As teachers we are very busy, but an occasional transcript is quite valuable to our own growth as writing teachers. Every time I think I've got it, I transcribe a session. I find that I am doing better, but that I am far from where I want to be, and back to the drawing board I go.

If we are not careful to listen to what our students have to say in writing conference, we are simply giving them a one-on-one version of Charlie Brown's teacher from *Peanuts*. These practices are definitely a waste of their time and ours.

A CLOSE-UP LOOK AT A CONFERENCE

I've mentioned several times now that questions and the types of questions asked are very important. Donald Graves (1996) splits the questions asked in writing conference into several different groups. These different types of questions perform different desirable functions in the conference:

Open conference

Follow the writer's information

Deal with basic structures

Deal with process

Reveal development

Cause a loss of control (p. 139)

Graves's detailed description of types of questions reiterates that the effectiveness of a writing conference largely depends on the questions that the teacher asks. My sessions became 100 percent more effective when I learned to ask, "How do you see your paper right now?" When my students answered, I immediately knew where they were in their writing process and what their major concerns were. Even those who looked dumbfounded and answered, "You tell me; you're the expert," could eventually be coerced into talking about their paper and the process they went through in order to write it. The key is to think of the paper as a reader would rather than as a teacher might.

Mike and I had been working together on a series of papers. He was in a course designed around writing argument. Mike was pretty comfortable with the conference concept and sailed right into telling me what his paper is about. (Note: This transcript has been edited to fit the purposes of this chapter.)

Mike: There's no additional research required for this one.

Urbanski: It is an argument?

Mike: Yes, again.

Urbanski: Again?

Mike:	Um humm.
Urbanski:	So you've done two papers now?

In the WRC I had to begin the conference by finding out what the students were working on. I was in an interesting position in that I did not assign or grade the papers that I worked with. Working with papers like these is more applicable to the high school classroom than one might first believe. When we are conferencing with students, we should not be concerned with the grade a student is going to get. We should be concerned with the point the student is in with that paper in that moment. Also, ideally, our students should be picking their own topics. Finding out what they mean to write about is integral to having a good conference.

Urbanski:	What have you, have you done anything on this yet?
Mike:	I have. I took my first paragraph from my other paper.
Urbanski:	Your exploration paper?
Mike:	Yeah.
Urbanski:	So it has to be on the same topic?
Mike:	Right, right. We're using the same wonderful thing.
Urbanski:	How do you feel about that topic?
Mike:	Um, actually I chose it because I thought I could write a whole lot about it. And that's what she wanted us to do so . . .
Urbanski:	And you feel like now you can write, do you still feel that way?
Mike:	Um yeah, I just got to get in the mood again.
Urbanski:	Okay.
Mike:	I just used the same general introduction. I did that copy and paste thing. And this is actually what I want to argue. *[Reading]* "The mixture of hard work and reward is the key for success. If the reward is given for hard work the student will work harder not only for the reward of a good grade, but for a reward from the teacher." I think this is actually an old copy. *[Reading]* "I have seen this in a kindergarten class." Yeah this is an old copy of it.

Urbanski: John and Susan?

Mike: John and Susan, I just copied this paragraph. That's actually what I want to argue.

Here Mike is telling me where he is in the process of writing this paper. He has already written an exploratory paper on the same topic in which he had to represent three different points of view. His comment, "the same wonderful topic," makes me think that he is sick of what he's writing about, but when I question him further he says that he just has to get in the mood again. As he continues to talk, I find that he has not really written very much new material at this point but simply cut and pasted from the old paper. His last statement, "John and Susan, I just copied this paragraph. That's actually what I want to argue," is a little confusing for me, so I go back and ask for some clarification.

Urbanski: So, go back, let me look at this for a minute.

Mike: Okay.

Urbanski: So your claim is mixing of hard work and reward is the key for success?

Mike: Right.

Urbanski: *[Reading]* "If a reward is given for hard work, students will work harder, not only for their own reward of a good grade, but a reward from the teacher also." That's your claim?

Mike: Um humm, pretty much.

Urbanski: That works for me. *[Referring to assignment sheet]* You have to have the claim.

I have given Mike back the information that he has given me in what he has written. He now knows that I can find the claim because I have read it to him. Still, his response to my question of it being his claim concerns me. He doesn't sound quite sure. We return to the assignment sheet for a moment to see what else he needs to have.

Mike:	You have to have the support.
Urbanski:	*[Reading]* "Specific examples, fact, opinion from excerpts in the three essays found in your reader." So you just use the stuff in there.
Mike:	Right.

Before I directly address the issue of his claim, I ask about his plans for the piece. Now that we have established what the assignment is, I want to know what he plans to do about it. I have to be very careful with Mike. He is a nice kid, but he is one of the students that he describes in his paper. He can get by on personality. He makes you want to help him, and he has found that if he looks confused for long enough, people will give him the answers instead of making him find them. He is now waiting for me to tell him how to set up his paper.

Mike:	*[Flipping through papers]* A lot of the support would actually be, he was actually joking when he said this. It's the same thing about giving kids . . . hang on, no that's what I'm going to use to argue. It was the stupid little quote he put in here that I wanted to argue.
	[Reading] "Having been raised on gold stars for effort and smiley faces for self-esteem, they find that they can get by without hard work and real talent if they can talk the professor into giving them a break." I want to argue that it's true.
Urbanski:	Okay, mark that in your book so that you don't lose it again. Okay, now, do you think that it would be better to just put that quote and try to argue it, or to put the ideas of that quote into your own words? Which do you think would be better?
Mike:	I'll leave the direct quote because I think, actually, that's a thought because, I don't know, because I don't think that I can put it into my own words.

He has decided to use a quote as a part of his support. It is obvious here that Mike trusts that I am not asking leading questions, because when I ask him about using the quote or putting it in his own words, he responds with what he genuinely wants to do instead of what he thinks I want to hear. Reading back over the transcript, I see the value of establishing trust with the student. I really was asking a leading question here; I didn't want him to use the quote. I messed up, but he didn't notice because it is not what I usually do. Saved! I realized what I was doing after he responded; so I began to feed back to him what he wrote. I was pretty sure that he did not completely understand the quote, based on my experience with the last paper he used it in, but I check to see if maybe he has had an epiphany.

Urbanski:	Oh, okay. *[Reads the quote again]* So what do you think all that means?
Mike:	That they can, um, not do any work at all and pray for a good grade pretty much.
Urbanski:	By? How do you get that good grade without doing the work?
Mike:	Persuasion.
Urbanski:	Persuasion, just being a nice kid?
Mike:	Um humm, a good kid. A good kid that looks like they're working hard, but they're not.
Urbanski:	Yeah, playing the game. Okay, so does this claim match with this?
Mike:	Um—no!

As Mike tells me what the quote means to him, he discovers that it does not support his claim. He comes to this knowledge on his own and therefore recognizes what he needs to work on. Had I simply read what he had written and told him that the claim did not match the support he was using, he might not have clearly understood why or even believed me, and he certainly would have lost ownership of his paper.

That last question I asked, "Does this claim match with this?" is what Graves (1996) means when he says that sometimes we need to ask questions that cause the writer to experience a loss of control (p. 139). He does not mean that we are taking control or ownership of the paper away from the students but that we are presenting them with a problem that they need to work with. I would like to add to this by saying that it should be a problem that we see as a reader, not necessarily as the learned teacher. As a reader, I did not understand the connection that Mike was making between his claim and the support he was using. He may very well have had an explanation for that. Had he, he would have been able to add that to the paper to help clarify the point for the reader. As it turned out, in this instance, he didn't, so he knows that he needs to either rework his claim or find a different support. In the 10 minutes that we chatted, Mike noticed that he needed to do more thinking about what he wanted to say. What he has written so far is confusing to his readers. He knows what he needs to do next. Most important, he came to that knowledge on his own, not because I said, "Do this!"

CONCLUSIONS

Dr. Sam Watson has said, "Writing floats on a sea of talk." For some writers, this talk takes place between their pens and the paper they write on, but for many of our students, it needs to be a conversation between people. Conferencing with students is one way to supply that talk.

But we must tread cautiously. In order to conference effectively with students, we must banish our teacher hats and secure our reader hats tightly so that the hot air of our own egos does not blow them away. We look at the students' writing as the coach watches a runner during a meet. The teacher becomes a trained spectator. We must admire the beauty of what the students are doing, and at times we will notice when they stumble and falter. As a trained spectator, we may sometimes notice what caused that faltering, and we can help the writer reflect on that. Other times, we may only notice the stumble. Then we work with the writer to find out the cause.

By talking with our students individually, we can understand each person's process and teach what he or she needs to know as he or she is ready for it. In doing this, we increase the amount of time that they spend actively learning rather than simply taking up space and waiting for the bell to ring. We also enable students to become independent in their writing as well as in their learning. They become active participants in their own education.

CHAPTER EIGHT

Becoming Independent

Writing and Literature Groups

O ur most important goal as teachers is to give students skills and ideas that they can use in life when we are no longer with them. Typically, at the end of the year they leave us for other classrooms that aren't set up the way ours are. They will be asked to write papers without teacher conferences or draft days. My runners will someday train for a 5K, 10K, or marathon largely on their own. Our hope is that our students will take what we've taught them, apply it to those situations, and soar.

The writing conferences that I discussed in the preceding chapter go a long way toward creating that independence in our students. Tom Romano (1987) states, "Experienced writers possess two voices. One dictates the flow of words; the second questions clarity and logic" (p. 91). As we question students in writing conferences, they learn what kinds of questions they need to be asking themselves as they write and revise. In the end, conferencing is just one more way we model for our students what writers really do.

We are also modeling questions that students can ask in order to help each other. Students *can* help each other with their writing. As they watch us respond to their writing, they can learn how to respond to each other's writing. After a while, they will have many people in their classroom to turn to for the response that Elbow (1973) reminds us we desperately need as writers.

Students also learn how to respond to each other's writing through discussion and exploration of literature. As students become more and more comfortable discussing literature in the way I described in Chapter 3, they will become more and more confident in their own judgment concerning what makes a good piece of writing (Calkins, 1986, p. 245). From here, it would be only a short step to enable students to see their own writing as literature. Next I will walk you through how these groups look in my classroom. If you would like to explore group work further, I have provided a list of the titles in the Suggested Reading at the end of this chapter.

A SCENARIO: STUDENT WRITING AS CLASS LITERATURE

After about a couple of months of school, students become quite comfortable with writing conferences. They are learning what kinds of questions help writers write and have come to see the value of a reader's response to their writing. They are also learning what kinds of things confuse the reader, and what kinds of things intrigue the reader and make him want to read more.

They are becoming more and more comfortable with literary discussion. They are becoming interested in how an author puts a piece of writing together and the choices he might make. They are coming to respect an author's right to make that choice, but also their own right to question that choice and disagree with it.

In short, students are beginning to think of themselves as readers and writers. At this point, the teacher passes around a typed copy of a piece written by an unknown author and tells students that it is their reading assignment. The next day in class, discussion ensues after the usual writing in reader response logs. The discussion is rich with students asking wonderful questions of the author and making excellent inferences about the author's purposes in composing the piece. There are also quite a few personal reactions and responses.

At the end of the discussion, the teacher reveals that the piece was actually written by a student in the class whom she has been in cahoots with all along. She then offers a brief explanation of how what the students write is, in fact, literature and will be treated that way by the class.

* * *

By using student papers as literature for the class, we not only give our students a forum in which to share their writing, but we also bring the connection between reading and writing full circle. Students are learning real purposes for both reading and writing. They are becoming each other's coaches and are needing us less and less.

Student Response to Groups

When I returned to the high school classroom and began conferencing with my students regularly, I wasn't terribly surprised that they felt the conference to be beneficial. I was, however, shocked at how valuable they began to find their writing and literature groups. They were, after all, just tenth graders. Their constant clamoring for me decreased exponentially over the course of the year as they grew to trust each other as readers and writers. Some even developed online writing groups of sorts when they needed a reader at odd hours in the night, when I was most certainly off duty.

I'd like to thank [the people in my writing group]. The opinions of others are invaluable to me. My writing groups have helped so much this year.

In the future, I believe that I will mainly rely on my teacher and my friends for bouncing ideas off of them. I would have had a lot more trouble this year had [the people in my writing group] not been there to tell me what they thought of my ideas and what they would change.

Writing groups are definitely God-sent. It was very nice to have 3 pairs of intelligent eyes looking over my work and making suggestions. . . .

Lit groups give me a place to bounce ideas I've had while reading and analyzing on my own off of others. My group can tell me if they think I'm on track or completely going in the wrong direction. I find that not only does working in lit groups solidify my understanding of the book, but they also show me several new ways to look at the work, that would never have occurred to me otherwise.

Literature groups allow you to sort through all of the ideas that pop into your head while reading a novel, because you know very well that your group members are probably just as confused as you are about the matter at hand. Being able to lay all of that confusion out on the table with a small group is very helpful in analyzing a novel, and you don't hesitate to do so as you would in a large discussion setting.

The literary groups that we use in class have helped a lot while reading every novel this year. Reading the books on our own, can be confusing, so it's great to have a group of people reading the same material to bounce ideas off of. As I read each section, I even made a list of questions and concepts I wasn't sure about, that I would bring to class specifically to ask my lit group about.

These are just a few of the comments that I found in year-end portfolios. But to me, more important than words were actions. As writing and literature groups became more and more valuable to students, the groups became more and more efficient. The groups began to stay on task with no prompting from me. They didn't want to waste time that they could be using to get feedback on their writing or figuring out a challenging piece of literature. They also refused to let each other get away with simply editing a piece or offering the cursory "That's good" comment and moving on. By Christmas, the groups were running themselves. They could even function with a substitute teacher. It was amazing!

HOW TO MAKE GROUPS WORK

Reading through what I've just written, my groups sound almost magical. In fact, that is how I always remember them at the beginning of each school year. And each and every year I am hit in the face with the reality that it takes quite a bit of work to get those groups functioning at that level. The usual happens. Students don't bring drafts. Students do bring drafts, but they have nothing to say about each other's work. Students bring drafts, do not trust their classmates, and want me to read each draft in class. Students spend most of their group time plotting an overthrow of the jock table at lunch. Students don't read. Students feel they have nothing to say about literature.

The truth is that for groups to work, the group members must buy into them. To get the group members to buy into them, we have to give them a reason to take each other's writing and ideas seriously and guidelines for giving good feedback. To set up high-functioning groups, you need to:

1. Model functional groups—often

2. Provide structure and incentive

3. Help students find their own structure

Model Functional Groups

Chapter 3 deals with the value of modeling, so I'll be brief here. I model writing and literature groups by drafting a few former students and a teacher friend of mine to come into my room and have a writing or literature group with me while the students watch. I try to keep the pieces short and interesting and keep the whole experience under 30 minutes. As they watch the writing group, students are responsible for writing down what they see happening. For classes that need a lot of structure, I may hand out an assignment that looks like this:

The Anatomy of a Writing Group

1. Describe in as much detail as possible what a writing group looks like.

2. What were the group members *doing*?

3. What types of body language did you see?

(Continued)

(Continued)

> 4. Who did most of the talking as each paper was discussed?
>
> 5. What did the listeners do?
>
> 6. What did the writers do?
>
> 7. What else did you notice?
>
> 8. Based on what you've seen here, what do you think a successful writing group needs?

The answers to these questions create wonderful large and small group discussions and give students incentive to pay attention to what is happening. The same form can be used to study a literature group by changing *writing* to *literature*.

Student groups also make great models throughout the year as well as in the beginning. It is helpful to the class to see a highly functioning group and talk about what makes it so, but it is equally as helpful to have a group that is struggling model so that the entire class can be in on the feedback process. As long as I have created an environment that allows for honesty and growth, working with a dysfunctional group can be one of the most effective things I do to set up groups in my classroom.

Provide Structure and Incentive

In the beginning, it is easy for students to see group time as free time, especially if they are not yet sold on the idea of real revision and craft in their writing or on the value of one another's ideas about what they are reading. Feedback from peers is going to have very little value for the student who wants to get the assignment completed as quickly as possible. Groups cannot work without all of the other concepts and ideas that we have discussed so far, and none of that sinks into a student overnight. To guide the process along in the beginning, I give assignments to both literature and writing groups that I take up and score. As time goes on and students show more ownership and independence with their groups, these assignments become more and more general and in some cases, with very mature classes, disappear altogether.

Writing Groups and Feedback Forms

Writing group assignments are called "feedback forms" in my class. Depending on the length of the writing students bring, each student fills out two to three forms per writing group. I take these forms and give students grades based on the amount of thought and detail they are putting into the answers to these questions. I return the forms to each writer so that they have their group members' comments to use as they revise. I record the readers' grades on an index card, with comments to be glued into their day-books. I also look at the forms a second time when I take up final papers to see how well students are using each other's advice. I do not expect students to give expert advice, but I do expect the advice to reflect application of the mini-lessons we have had in class as well as the conversations we have had about their own writing. For the most part, students who do their best to apply what we are learning and give thoughtful comments receive high grades.

What you see next is an example of a feedback form for the first draft of a personal essay assigned as the first paper of the year. Later, after we've worked with it a bit, I would change the wording for number 4 to "Are there any points where coherence breaks down?"

Reader's Name _____   **Writer's Name** _____

Writing Group Feedback Form—*Personal Essay*

1. Can you identify a main idea/purpose? What is it?

2. Describe the form of the piece and how it is working to support the main idea/purpose identified in #1.

3. What is the driving conflict of the piece?

4. Identify the best example of development/support of the main idea/purpose. Are there areas that could use more development/support?

5. Are there areas of the piece where the writer seems to jump from one topic to another with no transition? How might the author fix that?

6. What do you see as the strength in the piece?

The feedback form you see following is for the second draft of a short story students were writing, implementing all they had learned about the Dark Romantic Era.

Reader's Name _____   **Writer's Name** _____

Dark Romanticism Workshop

1. What is the overall message of the story?

2. What single effect does the other create and how does he/she do that?

3. Give examples of each element of Dark Romanticism in the story.

4. Look at the organization of the story. Does it have a beginning, middle, and end? Does it have more than one paragraph? If not, where might the writer create paragraphs?

5. What are the consequences of the main characters' actions?

6. What mood does the author set? How does he/she do that?

7. What symbols does the author use? What purpose do they serve?

I am using the Dark Romanticism feedback form not only to help students look critically at each other's writing, but to review many of the facets we have learned in this literature study. As the groups work with each other's papers, they are reviewing the elements of the Dark Romantic Era, the concept of single effect, and the basic structure of a short story.

In the final workshop before a paper is due, I ask students to respond to each other's papers using the rubric that I will be using to assess the piece. They are to give each other justification for the scores they give.

Silent Writing Groups

In the beginning, I require strict silence in these workshops. All communication among group members is through writing. This ensures that students can concentrate on what they read and forces them to put all response in writing so that the writer can have a reference when he returns to work on his drafts later. At the end of the allotted time, I give students 10 minutes or so to read over the responses they have received and ask clarification questions. As time goes on, students fall into this pattern on their own, and I am not as strict about time limits for each part of the process.

Literature Group Assignments

Assignments for literature groups vary a bit more than for writing groups. In the beginning, they are designed to help students generate deep discussion about literature and get feedback from me quickly on that discussion. My goal is to have each group member working and thinking together, so the divide-and-conquer method is not allowed. Unlike with the writing groups, silence here is a sure sign of trouble.

Each group member is expected to take notes on group conversation in their daybooks. One member of the group acts as the recorder by writing up the group's conversation on a colored piece of paper that I provide. I take one paper from each group, read and grade it, and return it to the recorder to glue into her daybook as her copy of the group's conversation.

Here are some samples of literature group assignments. Sometimes each group deals with the entire reading selection for the day.

What types of social commentary about classism, feminism, and racism in the South do you see in Section 1 of your reading in *Cold Sassy Tree?* Support your findings with very specific examples.

Other times each group takes a section to work with and then presents their finding in a large group. This works well with tough texts.

Literature Groups

The Visit Act I

Directions: Reread your scene carefully, and then break it apart for form and function as a group. Be sure to include all stage directions in your analysis, and begin to form some opinions about how you would stage it were you the directors. Pay close attention to literary devices, and support your analysis carefully and completely. The ultimate question of course is "What is the author doing and how does he *do* it?" The assignment will be graded using the IB Rubric.

Scene 1 Group 1
Waiting at the train station (pp. 11–16)

Scene 2 Group 2
Claire's entrance (pp. 17–20) to train leaving

Scene 3 Group 3
Introductions (pp. 20–25) Mayor's speech to the scene change

Scene 4 Group 4
Making plans (pp. 25–27) to scene change

Scene 5 Group 5
Setting it all up (pp. 27–35) through Mayor's speech

Scene 6 Group 6
The bargain revealed (pp. 35–39)

As students bond more and more in their groups and are ready for longer-term thinking with fewer checks, I assign whole book projects like the one you see here:

Literature Groups

Night by Elie Wiesel

Group 1

Literary Terms

Define each of the following terms and then give as many examples as you can find for each. Be sure to include page numbers. Discuss the effect the use of each of these devices has on your group as readers.

Simile	Allusion
Metaphor	Symbol
Personification	

Group 2

Historical Background

Research/represent the power structure used in concentration camps.

Research/represent one of the concentration camps Eli and his father were in.

Research/represent the Allied strategy from 1944 to the end of the war.

Show the historical accuracy of *Night* based on what you have found.

Use and document at least four sources, none of which may be encyclopedia.

Group 3

Looking for Messages in Literature

Examine the concepts of faith, hope, and religion in *Night*.

Use quotes and your own responses as you gather information about how these concepts are important in *Night*.

Group 4

Words of Power

Collect quotes in *Night* that carry great power.

(Continued)

(Continued)

Explain the power of each quote, the author's intent in using these words, and the effect of these words on the reader.

Group 5

Theme: Survival

Examine the concept of survival in *Night*.

Use quotes and your own responses as you gather information about how these concepts are important in *Night*.

Group 6

Theme: Man's Inhumanity to Man

Examine the concept of survival in *Night*.

Use quotes and your own responses as you gather information about how these concepts are important in *Night*.

Be sure to consider the roles of power and prejudice in connection to man's inhumanity to his fellow human beings and what kinds of things would lead human beings to act in this way.

As students work through these projects, they become responsible for planning *how* they will use their group time to accomplish their goals. They are also responsible for deciding how they will present their information and analysis to the class. By the time students complete a project like this one over several class periods, they are well on their way to independence.

As I create my literature group assignments, I am exposing my students to the many different things they need to think about as they study literature. These assignments are not merely critical thinking questions about specific texts, but different lenses through which literate people view print as well as nonprint text.

Help Students Find Their Own Structure

If our ultimate goal is for our students to be able to function independently in these groups, we have to let go of our control over the group over time. After students have met several times in their groups and have had success with them, it is important to give the students input into how they would like to run their own groups. For writing groups, I start this process by working with the entire class to set up feedback forms for upcoming workshops. As that becomes more and more successful, I have each group design their own form to turn into me for approval prior to the workshop. Finally, I let the groups decide how to use their time on any given day for any given workshop.

Some classes are able to operate in writing groups effectively on their own within a month of starting school. Others never become completely independent. Some classes are split. We have to watch our students, and be aware of what they need.

Literature groups gain their independence in much the same way. Eventually, I move away from assignments and toward what you see here with a study of Albert Camus's *The Plague* (1948).

Literature Groups

The Plague

Create a plan for your group's study of *The Plague*. Be sure to include homework assignments to be ready for the next group meetings (any day a reading assignment is due) as well as plans for those group meetings. You will have about 20 minutes each time, and you will need to turn in evidence of your study and discussion of the novel. The group's portfolio should consist of daybook photocopies turned in on the last day of discussion along with a reflection of the group's process.

** **Of COURSE all members will have notes on all discussions in their daybooks!**

With all of our focus on reading comprehension and literary terms, we are moving students toward three questions in their study of literature:

1. What is the author's purpose or goal?

2. How does the author achieve that purpose or goal?

3. Is what the author doing effective?

An understanding of these questions brings students to see the complete connections between their own writing and what they read and see. That connection creates truly independent thinkers and lifelong learners. Mission accomplished!

WHAT ABOUT THE KID WHO DOESN'T BUY INTO GROUP WORK?

In my class, group participation is an expectation, but that does not mean that every single student participates. There are a few reasons that a student is barred from a writing group:

1. No writing to share

2. Reader responses not completed

3. Group disruption

4. Lack of contribution

Students exhibiting any of the behaviors are immediately removed from the group and spend group time working alone or with me. Especially disruptive students are permanent fixtures in the fluid revision circles discussed in Chapter 7. A disruptive student sits close by while I am conducting individual conferences. Besides the fact that having that student in close proximity makes it easier for me to monitor her behavior, she learns a lot from what she is hearing, and I find out a good deal more about why she is not being successful in writing group. If it is a literature group day, the student uses the time to catch up on reading and responding and has the option of completing the group assignment alone.

In my experience, students grow tired of sitting with me day after day while their classmates work in groups. They return to groups and become functional members not only because lack of participation is affecting their grades, but because they see the rest of the class enjoying each other's writing and discussion and want to experience that as well. In nine years I have had one student who could never really function in a writing group. That student had many other issues besides what was happening to him in my classroom. In the end, we found that the most effective use of his time was to work on his own writing or reading during group time. It worked for him and has worked periodically for other students.

TIMING

How often our students participate in groups depends a lot on those students, what you are attempting to accomplish in your class, and your school's schedule. Generally, it takes the first 2–4 weeks of school for me to acclimate my students to our workshop-based classroom. For many students, it is different from anything they have ever experienced. We spend those early weeks gaining one another's trust and front-loading information about class procedures. Once we make it through that set-up phase, the schedule is two literature days and a writing day. As I mentioned in Chapter 7, that doesn't mean that we don't discuss literature at all on writing days or write at all on literature days; it just gives students a predictable way to balance their workloads. Most days in my class involve a group meeting.

Writing Groups

Typically, I have my students, no matter what level, take two pieces of writing through the entire writing process per quarter. For each piece of writing we have an invention/introduction day and two workshop days that include writing groups. When at all possible, I give both writing assignments at the beginning of the quarter, with one due at midquarter and another at the end of the quarter. This way, students can function more like real writers by working with the piece that they feel most inspired by at the moment and taking more time with a piece that is giving them trouble. By the second semester, when groups are typically functioning pretty well, students can choose which drafts they are bringing on writing group days.

I find that 30–45 minutes is sufficient time for most groups. It is better to leave students with not quite enough time than too much time on their hands. Ideally, as groups finish, students would drift away to begin revision, but I have never had this happen consistently.

I have to force students back into their seats and institute quiet time to get them to revise, but it is a *very* important part of a workshop day.

Literature Groups

Our literature study is as predictable as our writing. I try to cover two major works or clusters of shorter works per quarter. For each unit of study, I have an introduction day and three workshop days. Most of my assessments are take-home projects or presentations, so we don't really need a test day. I find that I can break up most readings into three chunks, the length of each chunk depending on where weekends fall and whether reading assignments are back to back because of our two literature days/ one writing day schedule. I do realize that some students read more slowly than others and that often there are activities outside of school that make reading difficult on any given night. For that reason, I hand out the required reading schedule at the beginning of each quarter so that students can read ahead as they need to. I also allow for reading time in class for my lower-level students. Sometimes they read silently, sometimes I read to them, and other times they read together in their groups.

I find that 20–30 minutes is sufficient time for literature groups. After that, they run out of things to say to one another. Sometimes I have a short, large group discussion before groups meet, and sometimes I let the groups meet first in order to prepare for the large group discussion. Often, I plan to schedule it one way and change my mind as students come in talking about the book. If they have a lot of questions, I'll start with large group. If I start with large group and they are having trouble making sense of their thoughts, I'll move to small groups first. The key, of course, is flexibility.

CONCLUSIONS

Small groups foster independence in our students. We can use the groups to build their confidence as well as their sense of responsibility for their own learning. Sometime around November each year, a group of students will stop me in the hall to tell me about the online chat they had about the book we are reading. I'll walk through the cafeteria and see a group of my students huddled over each other's papers. The plethora of e-mails that I receive each night filled with questions about literature or requesting a read of a draft will begin to slowly decrease. I *love* that time of year because I know that it is beginning. There will still be many bumps along the way when I will have to reign students back in and remind them of what we are trying to accomplish, and there will still be days when groups fall flat, but I know that we have made it through the first hurdle, and I know that students are beginning to internalize the skills that they will be using years down the road. I know that I am doing my job and accomplishing what I set out to do for my students, and with that knowledge, no state assessment or college entrance exam is threatening to me or to my students. We have all learned to fly.

SUGGESTED READING

Atwell, Nancy. (1987). *In the middle: Writing, reading, and learning with adolescents.* Upper Montclair, NJ: Boynton/Cook.

Daniels, Harvey. (2002). *Literature circles: Voice and choice in book clubs and reading groups.* Portland, ME: Stenhouse.

Elbow, Peter. (1973). *Writing without teachers.* Oxford, UK: Oxford University Press.

Epilogue

Why Teachers Coach

Dear Cindy,

I was not trying to upset you or was I talking about Scott I was trying to get some points across only because I love you. I know what. You are studying for a career things have not changed only a little wicked and a lot wiser and better. I could have had you Robert, John, Linda to copy and correct all errors, but I want you see it as is. You can, I can, we can do all things through Crist that we want too. People tell me all the time I would do so and so, but I can't afford it they afford what they want. We had president that didn't finish High School. I could have if I had wanted a chain of stores no I chose to have time for you instead of more work and money. In my younger days I worked 14 to 18 hours 6–7 days a week to get us where we are. 12 miles to day is the same length now as ever we just cover it faster the world is the same size we can now go around it quicker years ago it took a life time. As you go to teach your people don't teach them they have to have a degree they can get where they want too faster with and with it if they don't work they still will not get there the degree is only a crutch or a wheel or a tool to get it please don't hold that little fellow back just because he don't have the means at the time to get a degree incourage him and her to push and work for what he wants. I am thankful you don't have to come the way I did and I just hope and pray you will go as far from start as I have from mine if you do you have a lot of work to do after you degree you just think now you work hard. You said to ride a bus is not like it use to be you are right they are warmer, cooler, bigger and run a lot better and quieter and quicker. So they are more on time and walking still is not crawling. I would ask you to keep this and when you are 30 or more read it again all this is with love for you,

Love,
Pa

Teachers coach because they believe that *all* children can learn to read and write. They believe that there is no reason for a single child to slip through the cracks of our education system. Making excuses about why a child can't seem to learn is unacceptable, whether those excuses are something in that child's background or a faulty state assessment system. We simply must show our students *how* to learn. Classrooms that teach students to regurgitate the information given to them handicap students for the rest of their lives. Part of teaching is showing a child how to work through rough spots and overcome adversity. Part of teaching is patience.

If we mean to help all children in the way that they need to be helped, we must step out from behind our desks and coach them. There are so many people in the world telling our children that they can't succeed, we need to be a consistent voice telling and showing them that they can. We must encourage and advise, cheer and push. We must work right along with our students in order to remind ourselves of what they are going through. We must study and learn so that we can offer them the best advice possible, and we must observe them carefully in order to help them find their own strengths and weaknesses. Most of all, we must be unrelenting in our beliefs that our children will learn to learn, learn to write, learn to read, learn to run, learn to fly.

Looking at these neatly typed gleaming white pages piled beside my grandfather's scrawled letter on folded yellow legal paper, I know that I coach the students I teach because I knew a little boy with badly burned legs who learned to run like the wind. I see his eyes behind those of every student I teach, and I feel his presence each year when I step into a room full of new students. I hope he knows of all of the lives that he has touched and will continue to touch for years to come.

References

Achebe, Chinua. (1959). *Things fall apart.* New York: Anchor.

Allen, Janet. (1995). *It's never too late.* Portsmouth, NH: Heinemann.

Atwell, Nancy. (1987). *In the middle: Writing, reading, and learning with adolescents.* Upper Montclair, NJ: Boynton/Cook.

Brannon, Lil. (1983). The teacher as philosopher: The madness behind our method. *Journal of Advanced Composition, 4,* 25–32.

Calkins, Lucy McCormick. (1986). *The art of teaching writing.* Portsmouth, NH: Heinemann.

Clark, Roy Peter. (1987). *Free to write: A journalist teaches young writers.* Portsmouth, NH: Heinemann.

Conners, Robert J. (1981). The rise and fall of the modes of discourse. *College Composition and Communication, 32*(4), 444–455.

Daniels, Harvey. (2002). *Literature circles: Voice and choice in book clubs and reading groups.* Portland, ME: Stenhouse.

Dellinger, Dixie Gibbs. (1982). *Out of the heart: How to design writing assignments for high school courses.* Berkeley: University of California Press.

Dillard, Annie. (1989). *The writing life.* New York: Harper Perennial.

Elbow, Peter. (1973). *Writing without teachers.* Oxford, UK: Oxford University Press.

Emig, Janet. (1983). From the composing process of twelfth graders. In Dixie Goswami & Maureen Butler (Eds.), *The web of meaning: Essays on writing, teaching, learning, and thinking* (pp. 61–96). Upper Montclair, NJ: Boynton/Cook.

Fletcher, Ralph. (1993). *What a writer needs.* Portsmouth, NH: Heinemann.

Fletcher, Ralph. (1996). *Breathing in, breathing out: Keeping a writer's notebook.* Portsmouth, NH: Heinemann.

Fort, Keith. (1971). Form, authority, and the critical essay. *College English, 32*(6), 629–639.

Graves, Donald H. (1991). *Build a literate classroom.* Portsmouth, NH: Heinemann.

Graves, Donald. (1996). *Writing: Teachers and children at work.* Portsmouth, NH: Heinemann.

Hairston, Maxine. (1982). The winds of change: Thomas Kuhn and the revolution in the teaching of writing. *College Composition and Communication, 33*(1), 76–88.

Hesse, Hermann. (1951/1998). *Siddhartha.* (Stanley Appelbaum, Trans.). Minneola, NY: Dover Thrift Editions.

Keene, Ellin Oliver, & Zimmermann, Susan. (1997). *Mosaic of thought: Teaching comprehension in a reader's workshop.* Portsmouth, NH: Heinemann.

King, Stephen. (2000). *On writing.* New York: Scribner.

Kirby, Dan. (1981). *Inside out.* Upper Montclair, NJ: Boynton/Cook.

Knoblauch, C. H., & Brannon, Lil. (1997). *Rhetorical traditions and the teaching of writing.* Portsmouth, NH: Heinemann.

Lamott, Anne. (1994). *Bird by bird: Some instructions on writing and life.* New York: Anchor.

Locke, John. (1690/1997). An essay concerning human understanding. *Classics of philosophy.* Retrieved April 17, 2000, from http://www.rbjones.com/rbjpub/philos/classics/locke/index.htm

Milner, Joseph O'Beime, & Milner, Lucy Floyd Morcock. (1999). *Bridging English.* Upper Saddle River, NJ: Merrill Prentice-Hall.

Moffet, James. (1981). *Active voice: A writing program across the curriculum.* Upper Montclair, NJ: Boynton/Cook.

Morrison, Toni. (1987). *Beloved.* New York: Plume.

Murray, Donald M. (1990). *Shoptalk: Learning to write with writers.* Portsmouth, NH: Heinemann-Boynton/Cook.

Murray, Donald M. (1999). *Write to learn.* Philadelphia: Harcourt Brace College.

Probst, Robert. (1988). *Response and analysis: Teaching literature in junior and senior high school.* Portsmouth, NH: Heinemann.

Romano, Tom. (1987). *Clearing the way: Working with teenage writers.* Portsmouth, NH: Heinemann.

Rose, Mike. (1989). *Lives on the boundary: A moving account of the struggles and achievements of America's educationally underprepared.* New York: Penguin.

Tan, Amy. (2001). *The bonesetter's daughter.* New York: Penguin Putnam.

Weaver, Constance. (1996). *Teaching grammar in context.* Portsmouth, NH: Heinemann-Boynton/Cook.

Weaver, Constance. (1997). *Lessons to share on teaching grammar in context.* Portsmouth, NH: Heinemann-Boynton/Cook.

Wiesel, Elie. (1960). *Night.* New York: Bantam.

Index

**CORWIN
PRESS**

The Corwin Press logo—a raven striding across an open book—represents the union of courage and learning. Corwin Press is committed to improving education for all learners by publishing books and other professional development resources for those serving the field of PreK–12 education. By providing practical, hands-on materials, Corwin Press continues to carry out the promise of its motto: **"Helping Educators Do Their Work Better."**